one two & three color graphics Vol. II

P·I·E BOOKS

one two & three
color graphics

Printed in Hong Kong by **Everbest Printing Co., Ltd.**

P•I•E BOOKS

Villa Phoenix Suite 301, 4-14-6, Komagome,

Toshima-ku, Tokyo 170, Japan

Tel: 03-3949-5010 Fax: 03-3949-5650

ISBN 4-938586-93-2 C3070 P16000E

First published in Germany 1996 by:

NIPPAN/ Nippon Shuppan Hanbai Deutschland GmbH

Krefelder Str. 85, D-40549 Düsseldorf, Germany

Tel: 0211-5048089 Fax: 0211-5049326

ISBN 3-910052-69-X

Contents

序　　文

　　デザイン表現における印刷方法の中で、メジャーな存在である4色印刷へのアンチテーゼとして取りあげたこのテーマも、早くもVol. 2の登場である。Vol. 1の制作当初は耳慣れないタイトルのためか反応もやや弱かったが、今回は世界中から応募作品が殺到するほどになった。

　　なぜ今、[1, 2 & 3 Color Graphics] がクリエイターをそんなにも魅了するのか？私は大量の作品群を眺めながら、色数が少ないという「シンプルさ」自体にその理由があることを感じずにいられなかった。ある意味、「覆い」をはぎ取られたかの様なこの条件のもとで、デザインにおけるすべての要素は白日にさらされてしまう。例えば、色の組み合わせ、素材の形、位置、サイズ…etc. ちょっとした狂いがとても強調されてしまうのである。デザイナーにとって、とても高度な技量が要求される分野であることは間違いないであろう。だが反面、シンプルさゆえに特殊な手法をすんなり取り入れることができたり、また自分の欲求を簡潔に表現できたり…という点で可能性の大きなフィールドであるとも言える。今回、本書に収録された作品はそれを証明している。様々な手法のタイポグラフィー、Wトーン等の特殊技法、色構成の新鮮さ、ラジカルなレイアウト…まさにコンテンポラリーグラフィックスの実験場と化しているかのようである。

　　そのような斬新さの一方で、レトロな懐かしさや親しみやすさを持つ作品が多い点も興味深い。3色以内の印刷は、昔のグラフィックでよく見られ、また最近はフライヤー、グリーティングカード、ステーショナリー…というスモール・グラフィックスの分野でもよく使用されている。もともとは「コストを抑える」という理由が主であっただろう。しかし今はそればかりでなく、チープさの妙とでも言うような楽しい効果を好み、敢えてこの方法を選ぶデザイナーも増えているようである。例えば色数の少ない絵本で、そのシンプルさが、かわいらしさや親しみやすさを効果的に表現していたり、数十年前のポスター等の古い作品が、単純な色使いによってレトロな味を醸し出しているのを目にしたことはないだろうか。本書にはそんなイメージを放ちつつ、うまく現代風にアレンジされた作品も数多く掲載されている。

　　「最先端」と「レトロ」、反目する要素が入り混じった作品群を見ていると、大きな変換期を迎え「今までのシステムを破壊し新しいものを探そうとする動き」と「過去を振り返って今を確認しようとする動き」とが渾然一体となっている現代の世相を連想してしまう。変化の激しい時代に、シンプルな土壌で自由にデザインが楽しめるこの手法がマッチし高感度なクリエイター達の支持を得ているのだとしても何ら不思議はないだろう。

　　本書には、世界各地から寄せられた、魅力的な作品が満載されている。これからページをめくるあなたが、ますますグラフィック・デザインのとりことなってしまうことを確信している。

ピエ・ブックス

F o r e w o r d

Here, already, is the follow-up volume on an area of graphics that pits itself against the mainstream four-color process printing widely used in design work. The first volume got off to a slow start with a lower-than-expected response, which we put down to the unfamiliar title. For this edition, however, we have been deluged with submissions from all over the world.

Why should a book called *1, 2 & 3 Color Graphics* appeal so strongly to designers at the present time? Looking through the many contributions we received, we have concluded that the explanation lies in the very simplicity imposed by limiting the use of color. It requires, in a sense, a paring away of excess layers to expose all the basic design elements to scrutiny. Color combinations, the forms the different design elements take, position, size – any tiny flaw will become greatly exaggerated. There is no doubt that a high level of skill is required on the part of designers. But at the same time this simplicity opens up a field rich with possibility, as designers can make use of special techniques, or produce their desired effect in a concise and economical way, and the artwork reproduced here is testimony to this. All manner of typography techniques, special techniques in double tones, crisp color coordination, radical layouts – the whole book has the appearance of a laboratory of contemporary graphics.

It is fascinating that many of these submissions, while clearly up-to-date, nevertheless evoke a nostalgia and haunting familiarity that hark back to times past. Printing in up to three colors was common in graphics years ago, and is now often utilized once again for small-sized artwork such as flyers, greeting cards and stationery items. Originally it probably had much to do with keeping costs down, but these days there are more and more designers who actually prefer the fun effects of what we might call the enigma of what is cheap, and specifically choose this method of expression. For instance there are picture books printed in limited colors, and their simplicity enhances their charm and all-encompassing appeal. And who hasn't seen old posters, say, from thirty or forty years ago, that put over such a powerful sense of earlier times. This book projects many such images, and includes large numbers of designs presented in a satisfying, contemporary way.

Looking at the many designs that bring together conflicting elements in being both ultra-modern and deliberately dated, we may be reminded of our current phase of life approaching the turn of the millennium, in which there are tendencies both to abandon former systems in a search for something new, and yet to look to the past to reaffirm the present. This particular technique, allowing as it does unrestrained design grounded in a fundamental simplicity, is well suited to these times of upheaval. It is no wonder then that it has gained such wide favor among designers sensitive to such changes.

This volume is full of splendid examples of artwork contributed by designers all over the world. We are confident that as you now begin to turn its pages, you will be captivated by some of the best in graphic design.

P•I•E BOOKS

Vorwort

Hier ist bereits der zweite Band des Bestsellers über die Gestaltung und den Druck mit nur einer, zwei oder drei Farben. Diese Graphik- und Druckdisziplin steht mit dem meistverwendeten Vierfarbendruck im Wettbewerb. War es schwierig, das Material für den ersten Band zusammenzutragen, so war jetzt das Gegenteil der Fall. Nach der Publikation von Band 1 wurden wir mit Designs aus aller Welt nahezu überschüttet.

Warum spricht ein Buch mit dem Titel >> 1, 2 & 3 Color Graphics << gerade in dieser Zeit Designer so stark an? Beim Betrachten der vielen Gestaltungsarbeiten, die wir erhalten haben, kamen wir zu folgender Feststellung: Die Erklärung liegt in der Einfachheit, die durch die Einschränkung von Farben, erzielt wird. Dies erfordert, sich von der Vielschichtigkeit zu trennen und die grundlegenden Designelemente in den Vordergrund zu stellen. Die Kombinationen von Farben, die verschiedenen Formen, die Designelemente bilden können, Stand und Größe - jedes kleine Designelement wirkt hier besonders stark. Ohne Zweifel wird von den Designern ein hohes Niveau an Fachwissen und Gestaltungstalent verlangt. Aber gleichzeitig öffnet die Einfachheit ein weites Feld von Möglichkeiten, denn der Designer kann sich spezieller Techniken bedienen. Der gewünschte Effekt läßt sich besonders ökonomisch erzielen, was die hier vorgestellten Arbeiten bezeugen : Kunstfertige Typographie, spezielle Drucktechniken wie Duotone, frische Farbkombinationen, radikale Layouts - das ganze Buch vermittelt den Eindruck einer Experimentierstätte des zeitgenössischen Graphik-Designs.

Es ist faszinierend, daß viele der eingereichten Arbeiten, obwohl sie hochaktuell sind, ein Gefühl der Nostalgie vermitteln. Sie spielen mit einem Wiedererkennen, das weit in die Vergangenheit zurückreicht. Mit ein bis drei Farben zu gestalten und zu drucken war im Graphik-Design vor vielen Jahren üblich. Es wird jetzt für kleinformatige Arbeiten wie Flyer, Grußkarten und Geschäftsausstattungen wiederentdeckt. Ursprünglich war der hauptsächliche Grund, die Kosten niedrig zu halten, aber heute erkennen mehr und mehr Designer die unterhaltsamen Effekte, die so erzielt werden können. Man kann es auch das Enigma des Billigen nennen. Sie wählen es ganz bewußt als Ausdrucksform. So werden zum Beispiel Bilderbücher mit wenigen Farben gedruckt. Die Einfachheit verstärkt ihren Charme und ihre allumfassende Attraktivität. Und wer hat nicht einmal Poster gesehen, 30 oder 40 Jahre alt, das solch ein kraftvolles Gefühl aus früheren Zeiten vermitteln. Dieses Buch zeigt viele solcher Arbeiten, bringt darüberhinaus aber auch eine Vielzahl von Designs in einem ansprechenden, zeitgemäßen Stil.

Wenn man die zahlreichen Designs betrachtet, die kontrastierende Elemente zusammenbringen, um gleichzeitig ultramodern und in der Vergangenheit verwurzelt zu sein, werden wir an unsere eigene Situation zum Ende des Jahrhunderts erinnert. Sie zeichnete sich dadurch aus, daß das bisherige System zurückgelassen wurde, um etwas Neues zu suchen und dennoch der Blick in die Vergangenheit die Gegenwart bestätigte. Diese besondere Technik, die unbeschränkte Designs von fundamentaler Einfachheit erlaubt, ist jetzt für unsere Zeit des Umbruchs speziell geeignet. Und es ist daher kein Wunder, daß sich viele Designer, die für solche Veränderungen ein Gespür haben, ihrer bedienen.

Dieses Buch ist mit vielen hervorragenden Gestaltungsbeispielen von Designern aus der ganzen Welt gefüllt. Wir sind sicher, daß, wenn Sie sich jetzt die Arbeiten betrachten, Sie von einigen der Designs regelrecht gefesselt sein werden.

P•I•E BOOKS

Editorial Notes

Credit Format
クレジット・フォーマット

AD: Art director   CD: Creative director

CL: Client   CW: Copywriter

D: Designer   DF: Design firm

I: Illustrator   PD: Producer   PH: Photographer

Submittor's nationality   出品者国籍

Year of completion   制作年度

Item（except POSTERS, MAIL）

アイテム名（目次 [POSTERS], [MAIL] を除く）

Color Samples
カラー情報について

For reference purposes, color samples of printing inks used in the artwork are shown on the same page. For this, information was mostly supplied by contributors, but in cases where insufficient information was provided, the editors have made their own judgement. Special effects and specialty inks are indicated by the code letters shown below.

出品者から送付された情報をもとに、作品に使用された印刷インクの参考資料として、各ページ端に「色サンプル」を掲載しました。出品者からの情報が不足している一部作品については小社で判断しました。また、再現が難しい特殊インクについては下記記号で表記しました。

- •Copper 銅 - C　•Fluorescent ink 蛍光色 - F
- •Gold 金色 - G　•Hot stamps 箔押し - H
- •Matte black マット黒 - MB
- •Metallic ink　パールインク - M　•Silver 銀色 - S
- •Thermography バーコ印刷 - T
- •Varnish/clear varnish/matte varnish ニス - V

This publication has been printed using standard four-color process inks, and there may be some slight variations in the printing of color samples.

本書は4色のプロセスカラーで印刷されていますので、「色サンプル」は実際の印刷インクとは多少異なる参考程度の情報であることをご了承下さい。

8 may
agurk
player(s)
+ party
with dj simon
richmond (uk)

the saturdays
at halles de
schaerbeek
koninklijke ste-mariastraat 22
rue royale ste-marie - 1030 bxl

before 12 pm: 250f - after 12 pm: 300f
doors: 10 pm - info: 02 513.88.18

D: Olivier Vandervliet / Nathalie Pollet DF: POP X Studio CL: Addison de Wit / Halles de Schaerbeek Belgium 1993

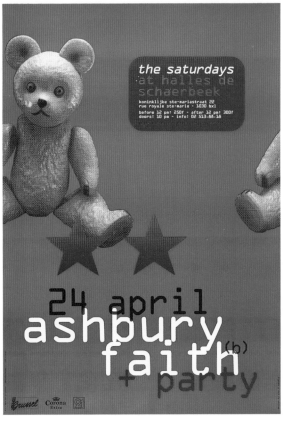

D: Olivier Vandervliet / Nathalie Pollet   DF: POP X Studio   CL: Addison de Wit / Halles de Schaerbeek   Belgium   1993

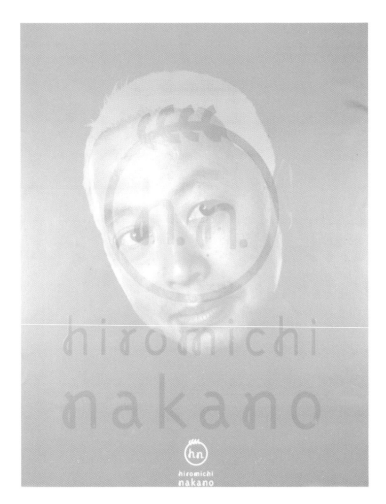

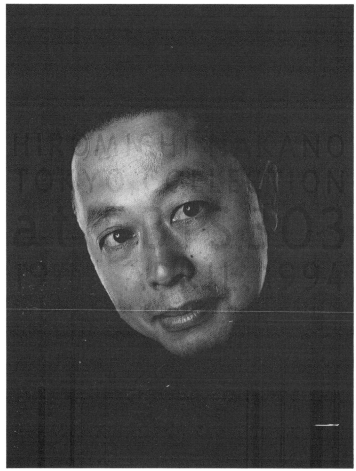

CD: Hiromichi Nakano AD, D: Katsunori Aoki PH: Yoshihito Imaizumi CL: Hiromichi Nakano Design Office Co., Ltd.   Japan   1994

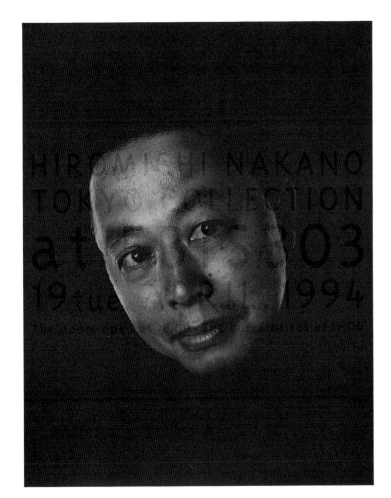

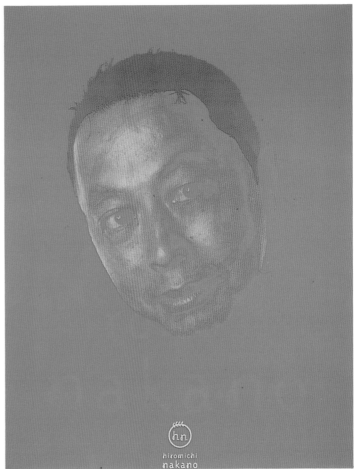

CD: Hiromichi Nakano AD, D: Katsunori Aoki PH: Yoshihito Imaizumi CL: Hiromichi Nakano Design Office Co., Ltd.   Japan   1994

CD, AD, D, DF: Ralph Schraivogel PH: Peter Lüem CL: Zürich Museum of Design   Switzerland 1993

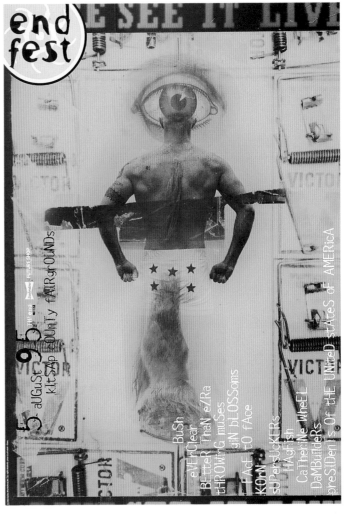

AD: Scott Wadler D: Timorse PH: Alicia Exum DF: MTV Networks CL: The End 107.7 FM USA 1995

AD: Hiroshi Nakajima DF: Plank CL: Röntgen Kunst Institut Von Katsuya Ikeuchi Galerie AG   Japan   1994

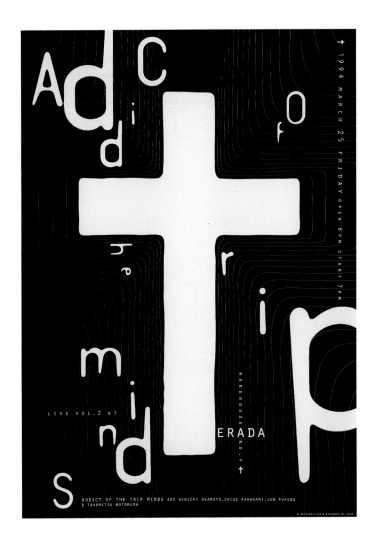

1. AD: Nobukazu Iida D: Yoshitaka Sato DF: GAGA Design Works CL: Gain You Inc.   Japan 1994

2. CD: Noi Sawaragi AD: Hiroshi Nakajima DF: Plank CL: Röntgen Kunst Institut Von Katsuya Ikeuchi Galerie AG   Japan 1995

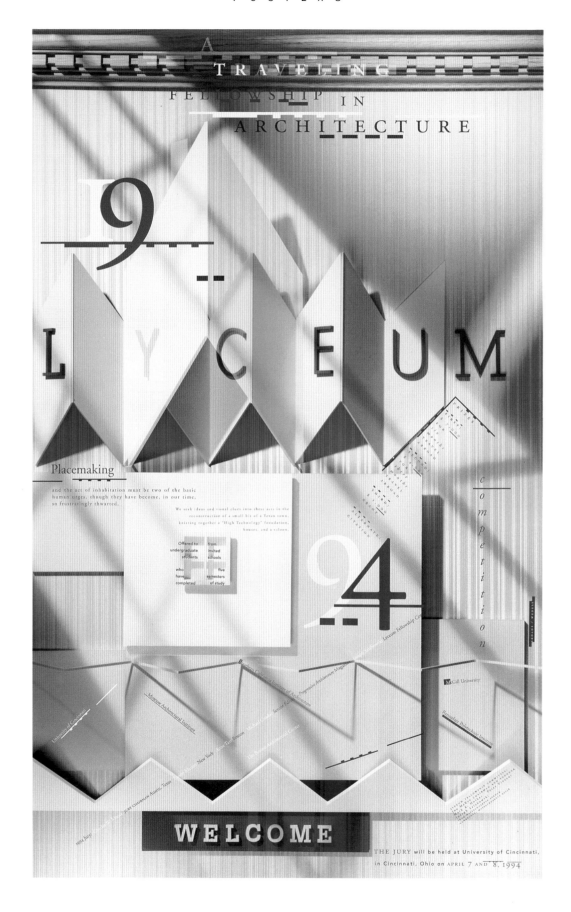

CD, D: Nancy Skolos PH: Thomas Wedell DF: Skolos/Wedell, Inc. CL: Lyceum Fellowship Committee   USA 1994

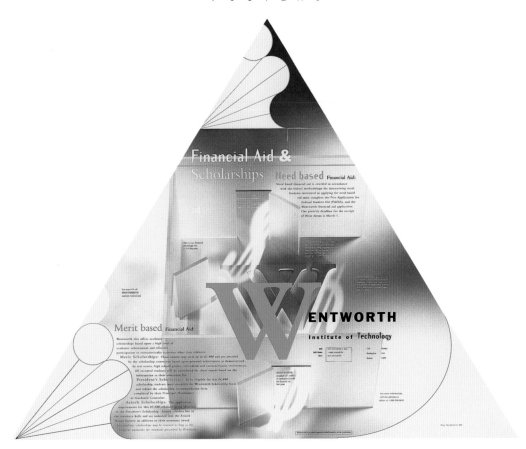

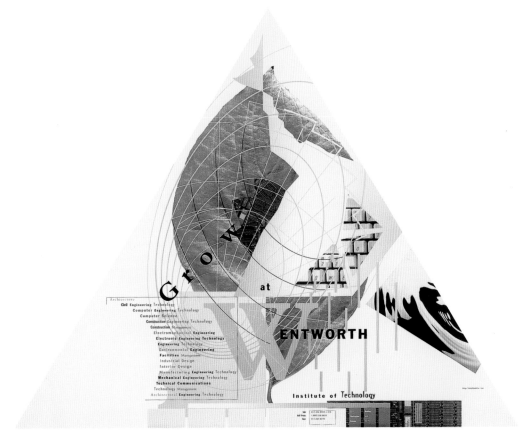

1. CD, D: Nancy Skolos PH: Thomas Wedell DF: Skolos/Wedell, Inc. CL: Wentworth Institute of Technology   USA   1995

2. CD, D: Nancy Skolos PH: Thomas Wedell DF: Skolos/Wedell, Inc. CL: Wentworth Institute of Technology   USA   1994

HU
MAN
rights*

* 1789, 1948, 1994..?

CD, AD, D: Haymo Kindler   DF: C. C. E   CL: Museum of Human Rights   France   1995

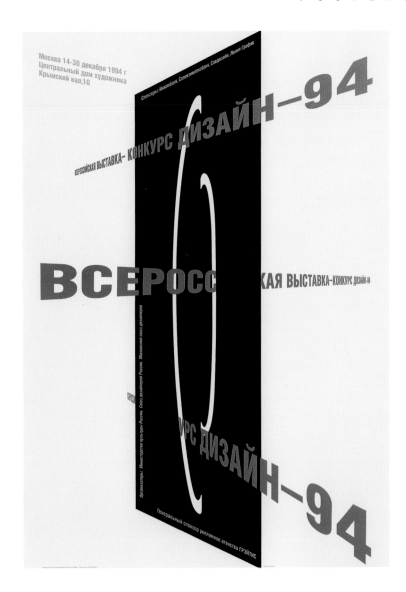

1. CD, AD, D, I: Yuri Surkov DF: Suric Design CL: Design Union of Russia Russia 1994

2. CD, D: Kurt Dornig DF: Dornig Grafik Design & Illustration Austria 1994

CD: Alexander Husson AD, I: Tim Murphy DF: POAGI® CL: 3d Radio   Australia   1994

Continuing
Professional
Development
Made Easy
Guidelines

An introduction to a new policy initiative by the Chartered Society of Designers

The Chartered Society of Designers supported by Interface

Interface Europe Ltd.

CD, D, I: Peter Grundy DF: Grundy & Northedge CL: CSD UK 1995

IN EVERY CLASS, IN EVERY SCHOOL, IN EVERY CITY, IN EVERY STATE. GAY, LESBIAN, BISEXUAL, TRANSGENDER AND QUESTIONING YOUTH ARE EVERYWHERE. YOU COUNT. REACH OUT. GET SUPPORT.

THE SEXUAL IDENTITY FORUM IS A SAFE, SUPPORTIVE AND CONFIDENTIAL DROP IN GROUP FOR GAY, LESBIAN, BISEXUAL, TRANSGENDER AND QUESTIONING YOUTH IN SAN MATEO COUNTY. (415) 572-0535

1. CD, AD, D: John Bielenberg D: Allen Ashton / Teri Vasarhelyi DF: Bielenberg Design CL: Sexual Identity Forum   USA 1994   F M ●

2. CD: Trevor Myles D, I: Rian Hughes DF: Device CL: Million Dollar Corporation   UK 1993   F ●

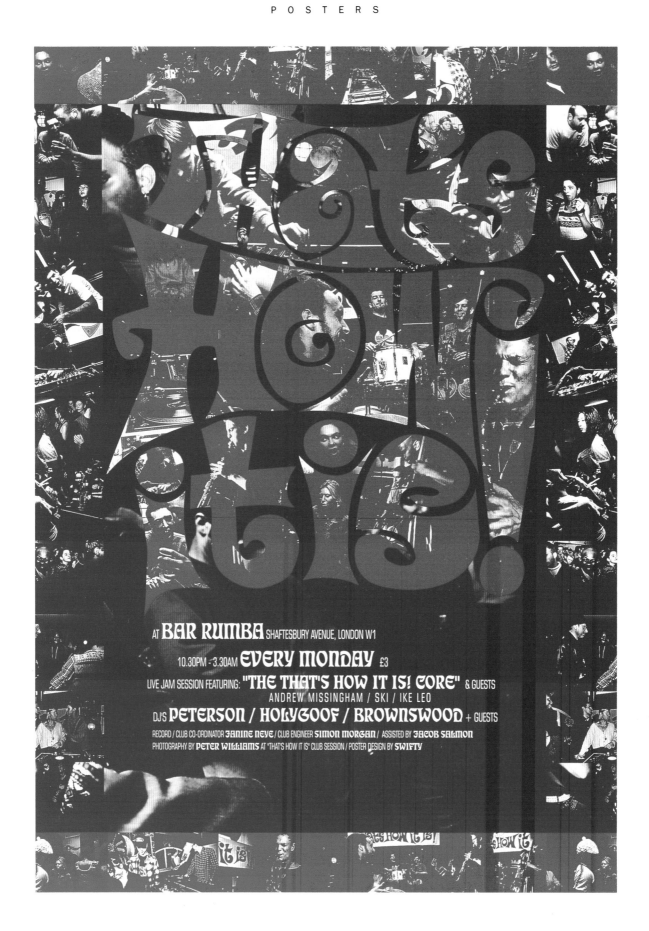

AT **BAR RUMBA** SHAFTESBURY AVENUE, LONDON W1

10.30PM - 3.30AM **EVERY MONDAY** £3

LIVE JAM SESSION FEATURING: "THE THAT'S HOW IT IS! CORE" & GUESTS
ANDREW MISSINGHAM / SKI / IKE LEO

DJ'S **PETERSON / HOLYGOOF / BROWNSWOOD** + GUESTS

RECORD / CLUB CO-ORDINATOR **JANINE NEYE** / CLUB ENGINEER **SIMON MORGAN** / ASSISTED BY **JACOB SALMON**
PHOTOGRAPHY BY **PETER WILLIAMS** AT "THAT'S HOW IT IS" CLUB SESSION / POSTER DESIGN BY **SWIFTY**

CD, AD, D: Swifty PH: Peter Williams DF: Swifty Typografix CL: "That's How It Is" UK 1994

AD: Nobukazu Iida D: Koichi Takahashi DF: GAGA Design Works CL: Gain You Inc.   Japan   1994

1. CD: Norimizu Ameya AD: Hiroshi Nakajima DF: Plank CL: Rötgen Kunst Institut Von Katsuya Ikeuchi Galerie AG   Japan 1993

2. CD, AD, D, PH:Kevin Helas DF: Helas Design CL: Artspace   New Zealand 1994

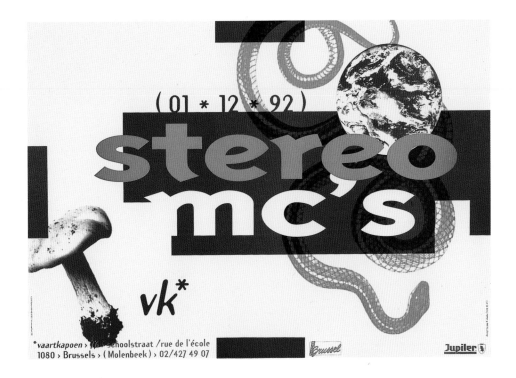

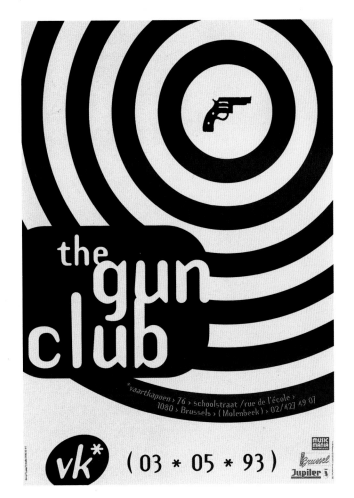

1. D: Oliver Vandervliet / Nathalie Pollet DF: POP X Studio CL: Vaartkapoen   Belgium   1992

2. D: Olivier Vandervliet / Nathalie Pollet DF: POP X Studio CL: Vaartkapoen   Belgium   1993

CD, AD, D, DF: Sigi Ramoser D: Stefan Gassner CL: Vorarlberer Landesregierung Austria 1995

1. D: Hiroshi Nakajima   DF: Plank   CL: NTT   USA   1993

2. CD: Mary Jo Ordrejka   AD, D: Ramona Hutko   DF, CL: In-house design by Presentations and Publications Department for Computer Sciences Corporation   USA   1994

AD, D: Masayoshi Nakajo CL: THE GINZA Co., Ltd. Japan 1994

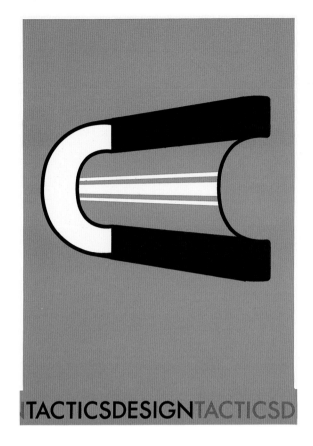

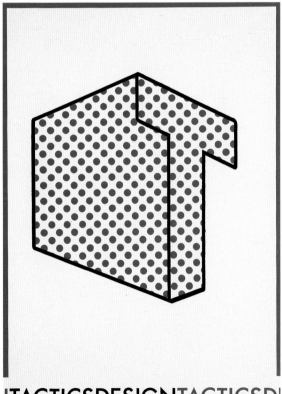

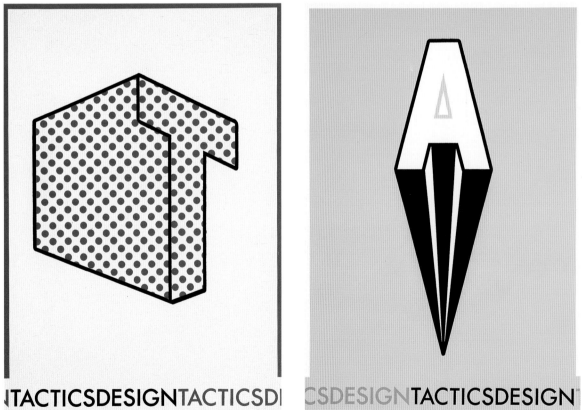

AD, D: Masayoshi Nakajo CL: THE GINZA Co., Ltd.   Japan   1994

MB

1. CD, AD, D: Tadeusz Piechura DF: Atelier Tadeusz Piechura CL: Galeria Manhattan   Poland   1993

MB

2. CD, AD, D: Tadeusz Piechura DF: Atelier Tadeusz Piechura CL: Medical University of Lodz   Poland   1993

1. CD, AD, D: Tadeusz Piechura DF: Atelier Tadeusz Piechura CL: Teatr 77 W Lodzi   Poland   1993

2. CD, AD, D: Tadeusz Piechura DF: Atelier Tadeusz Piechura CL: L D K-Community Centre   Poland   1994

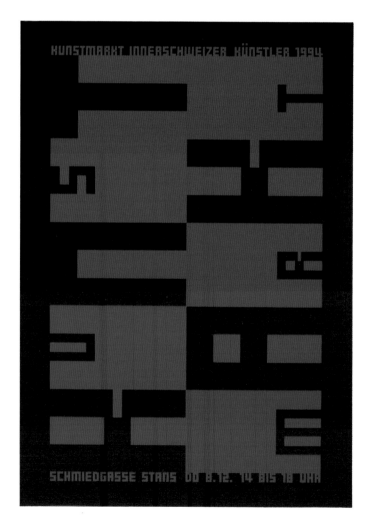

1. CD, AD, D: Imboden Melchior DF: Imboden Melchior, Grafic Studio CL: Art Galerie, Chaslager Stans Switzerland 1992

2. CD, AD, D: Imboden Melchior DF: Imboden Melchior, Grafic Studio CL: Art Galerie, Chaslager Stans Switzerland 1994

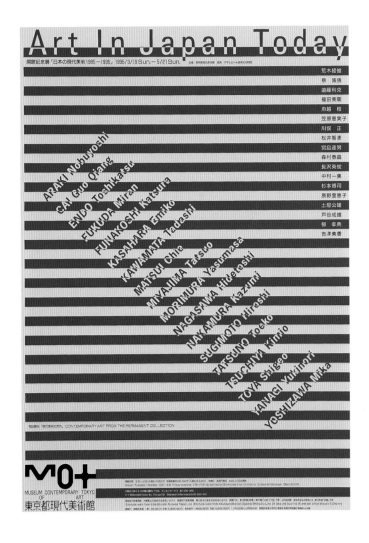

1. AD, D: Masayoshi Nakajo CL: The Ginza Co., Ltd.   Japan   1995

2. AD, D: Masayoshi Nakajo D: IMEX CL: Museum of Contemporary Art Tokyo Japan   1995

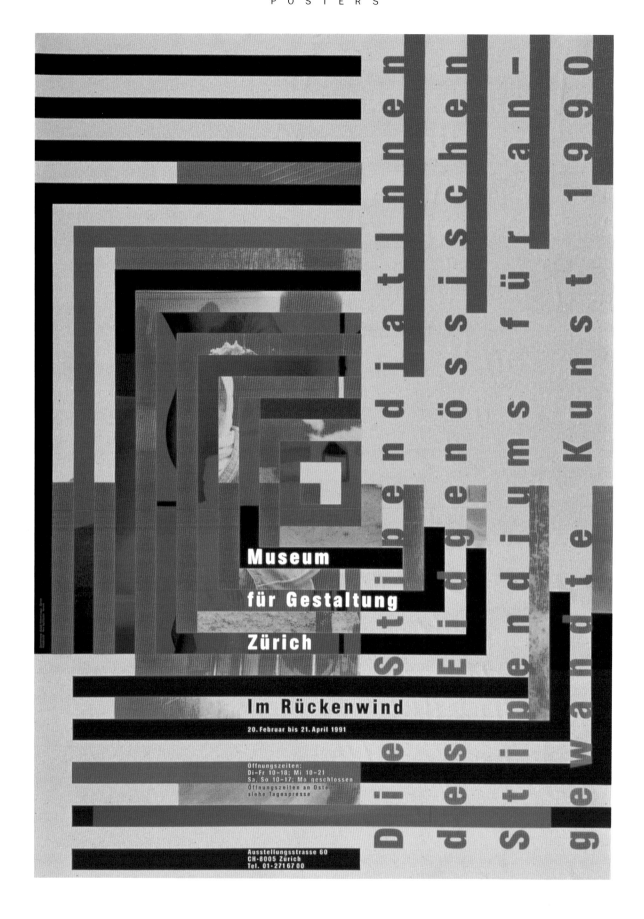

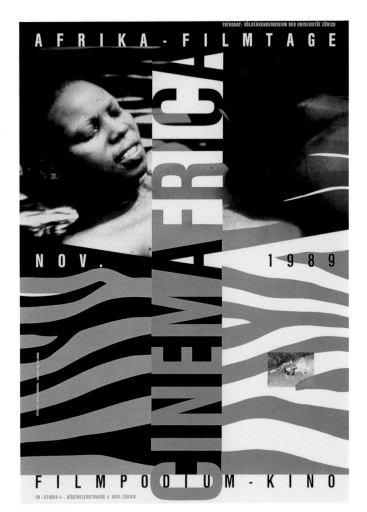

1. CD, AD, D, DF: Ralph Schraivogel CL: Looknow Switzerland 1990

2. CD, AD, D, DF: Ralph Schraivogel CL: Filmpodium Zürich Switzerland 1989

1995年4月5日(水)─4月21日(金)
会場＝上野公園・都美術館
入場時間＝9:00─16:00　休館日＝4月17日(月)
初日(正午開会)　最終日14:00閉会(入場は13:00まで)

公募　搬入日時＝4月1日(土)・2日(日)10:00─16:00
　　　搬入点数＝1人1点　出品料＝8,000円

社団法人　日本彫刻会
〒169東京都新宿区高田馬場1-29-18
レジョン・ド・諏訪202　TEL:03-3209-1861

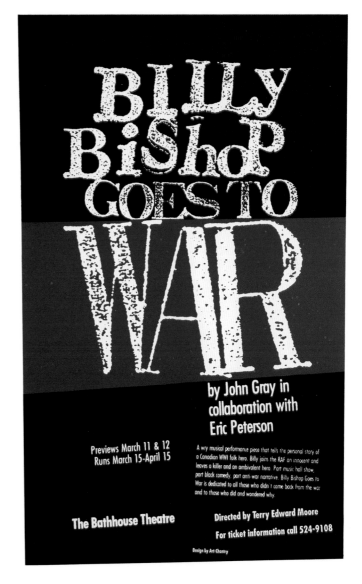

1. CD, AD, D: Leslie Chan Wing Kei DF: Leslie Chan Design Co., Ltd.   Taiwan 1995

2. D: Art Chantry DF: Art Chantry Design CL: The Bathhouse Theatre   USA 1995

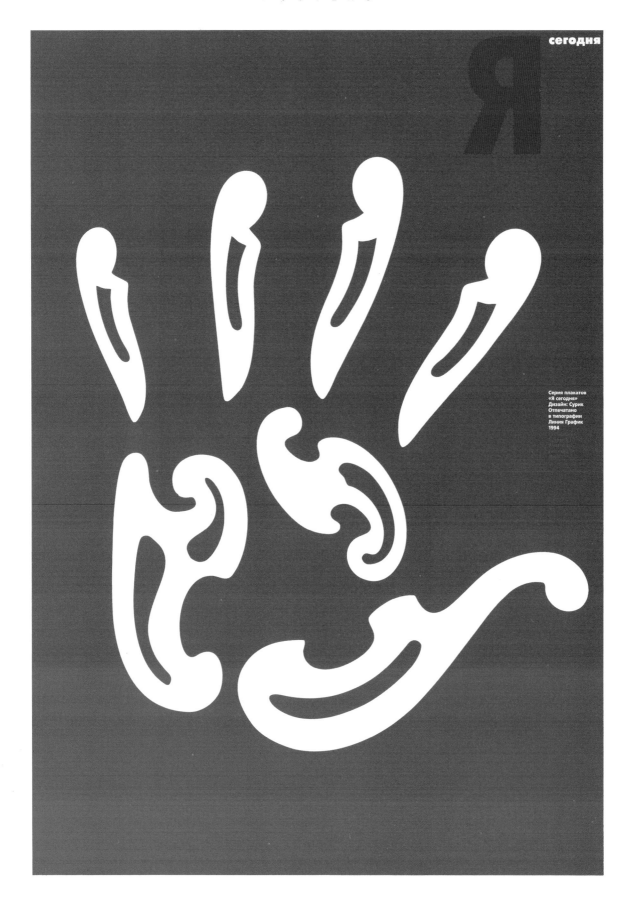

Серия плакатов
«Я сегодня»
Дизайн: Сурик
Отпечатано
в типографии
Линия График
1994

CD, AD, D, I: Yuri Surkov   DF, CL: Suric Design   Russia   1994

**Columbia University
Graduate School of Architecture
Planning and Preservation**

A One-Day Conference
presented by the PhD Students
of Urban Planning

CyberSpace

Public Space

HyperGhetto

New
Conceptions
of
Urban
Space

**Friday, October 14
Columbia University
Avery Hall
Wood Auditorium
116th Street/Broadway**

8:30am   Coffee

9:15   Welcome

9:30   **Opening Speaker**
         Susan Fainstein, Professor of Urban
         Planning and Policy Development,
         Rutgers University; author of
         *City Builders: Property, Politics & Planning
         in London and New York*
         Presentation: "Speculators and Space"

10:00   **The HyperGhetto**
         Featured Speaker: Loic Wacquant,
         Assistant Professor of Sociology,
         U.C. Berkeley
         Presentation: "The Hyperghetto as
         Structure and Practice"

         Respondent:
         Janet Abu-Lughod, Professor of Sociology,
         New School for Social Research

         Juried Presentations by Graduate Students

         Discussion

12:00pm Lunch Break

1:00   **The Urban Body**
         Featured Speaker: Richard J. Sennett,
         Professor of Humanities, New York
         University; author of *Flesh and Stone:
         a History of the Body in Western Civilization*
         Presentation: "The Passive Body"

         Moderator: Elliott Sclar
         Professor of Urban Planning,
         Columbia University

         Juried Presentations by Graduate Students

         Discussion

3:30   **CyberSpace**
         Featured Speaker: William Mitchell,
         Dean of Architecture, MIT
         author of *City of Bits: Space, Place and the
         Infobahn* (forthcoming)
         Presentation: "Cyborg Civics"

         Moderator: Saskia Sassen
         Professor of Urban Planning,
         Columbia University

         Juried Presentations by Graduate Students

         Discussion

6:00   Reception

         Information:
         212 932 3644
         email rfm9@columbia.edu

CD, D: Willi Kunz I: Tom Cox DF: Willi Kunz Associates, New York CL: Columbia University USA 1995

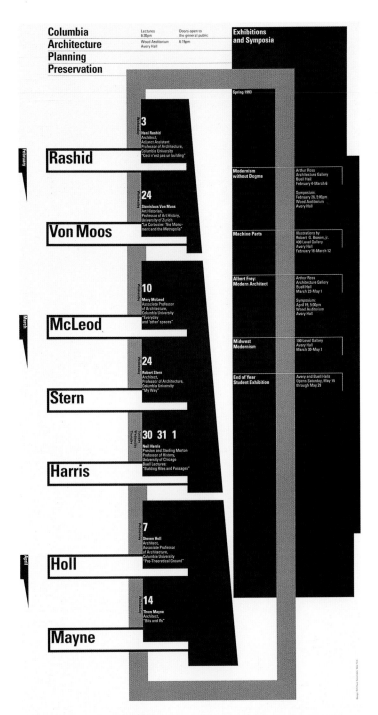

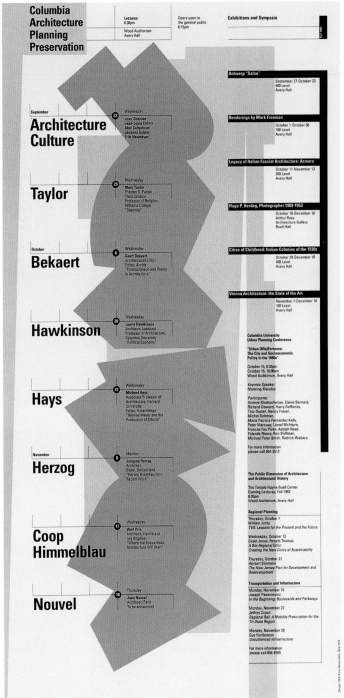

1. CD, D: Willi Kunz DF: Willi Kunz Associates, New York CL: Columbia University   USA   1993

2. CD, D: Willi Kunz I: Tom Cox DF: Willi Kunz Associates, New York CL: Columbia University   USA   1993

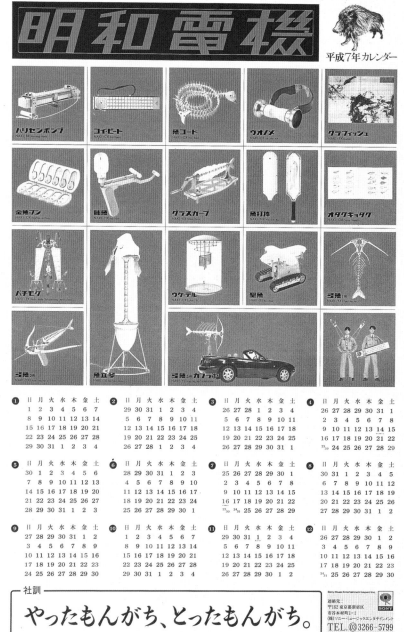

2, 3. CD: Norio Nakamura AD, D: Hiromi Watanabe CL: Sony Music Entertainment (Japan) Inc.   Japan

1. AD: Norio Nakamura D: Hiromi Watanabe Art: Maywa-Denki I: Kentaro Otani CL: Sony Music Entertainment (Japan) Inc.   Japan 1989

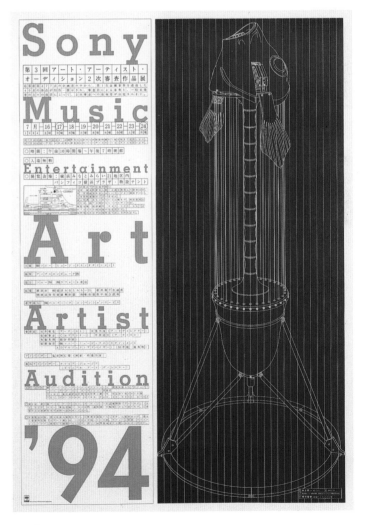

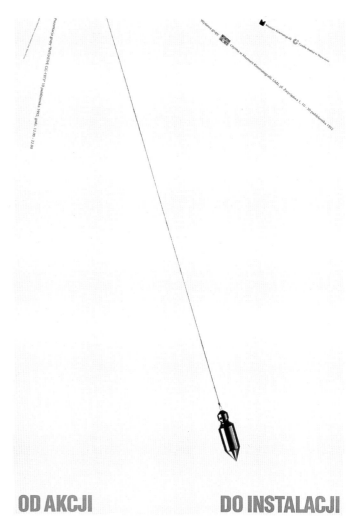

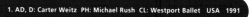

1. AD, D: Carter Weitz PH: Michael Rush CL: Westport Ballet   USA   1991

2. CD, AD, D: Tadeusz Piechura DF: Atelier Tadeusz Piechura CL: Museum of Cinematography   Poland   1992

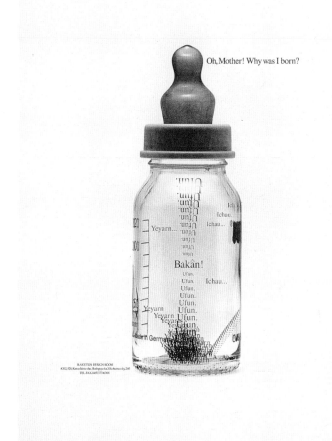

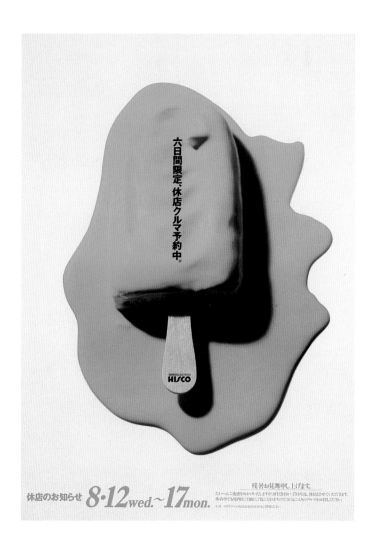

1. AD, D: Keisuke Kimura D: Maki Yanagishima PH: Naohiro Isshiki CL: Rakuten Design Room   Japan 1995

2. CD, CW: Kozo Koshimizu AD: Setsue Shimizu D: Shigeru Kanematsu PH: Takashi Shima PD: Eikatsu Seki DF: Hyper / C' CL: Honda International Sales Co., Ltd.   Japan 1992

CD, AD, D, DF: Ralph Schraivogel CL: Filmpodium Zürich Switzerland 1991

CD, AD, D, DF: Ralph Schraivogel CL: Filmpodium Zürich   Switzerland 1993

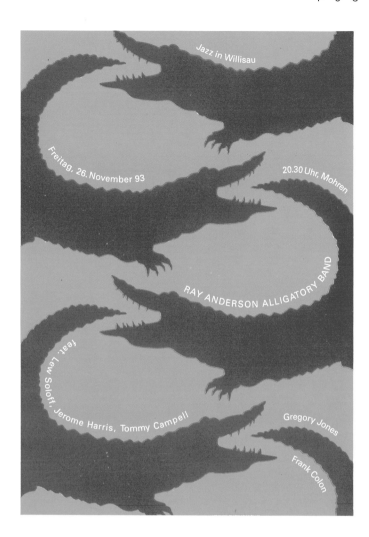

1. CD, AD, D, I: Niklaus Troxler **DF:** Niklaus Troxler Grafik **CL:** Jazz in Willisau   Switzerland   1993

2. CD, AD, D, I: Niklaus Troxler **DF:** Niklaus Troxler Grafik **CL:** Jazz in Willisau   Switzerland   1995

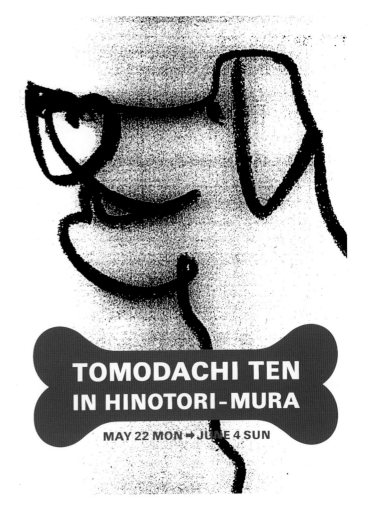

1. CD, AD, D, I: Niklaus Troxler DF: Niklaus Troxler Grafik CL: Jazz in Willisau   Switzerland 1990

2. CD: Hiroyoshi Hidaka AD, D: Eiichi Sakota D, I: Toshio Kawakami DF: Rec 2nd. CL: Hidaka Office   Japan 1995

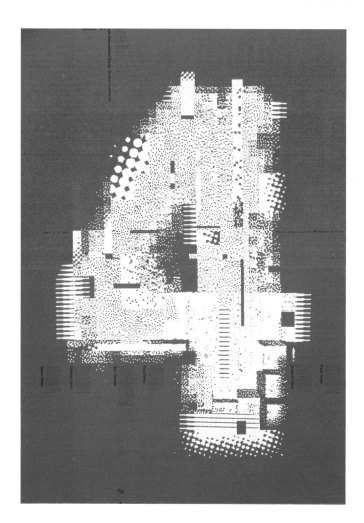

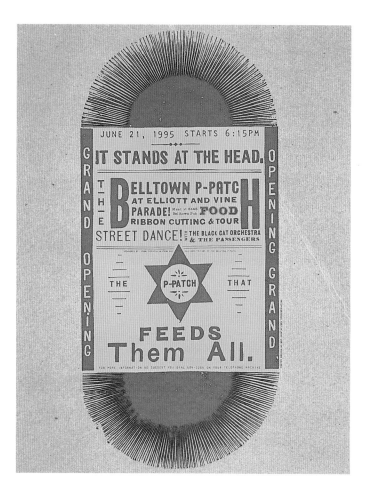

1. CD, AD, D, DF: Cato Design Inc. CL: Design Foundation Ltd. / Cato Design   Australia   1993-95

2. D: Art Chantry DF: Art Chantry Design CL: The Belltown P-Patch   USA   1995

SHREDDED OLLIE

two of New Yorks' leading exponents of experimental music of the last decade
on tour in New Zealand

Ikue Mori, Japanese/New York raw-tech percussionist,
drum machine pioneer. Downtown icon from the New York
improvisation scene. Member of cult group DNA and
collaborator with Fred Frith, John Zorn & Derek Bailey.

David Watson, expatriot New Zealander creator of "aural map
networks" using guitars' instrumental history, its various
vernaculars and its purely sonic/noise possibilities.

w w h i i   r l   d t o   u   r

performances by IKUE MORI & DAVID WATSON

genre bending sounds from the New York underground

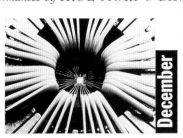

7	8pm	ARTSPACE, Auckland, First Floor 6-8 Quay St
8	6pm	City Gallery, Wellington (with 'Dress')
15	7.30pm	Suter Gallery, Nelson
17	8pm	Govett-Brewster Art Gallery, New Plymouth

"often inspired, sometimes amusing, but always urbane
....savvy invention" New York Times

"pure noise joy" Musician Magazine

with the assistance of the Arts Council of New Zealand/Toi Aotearoa

1. D, I: Mark Fox DF, CL: BlackDog USA 1994

2. CD, AD, D:Kevin Helas DF: Helas Design CL: Artspace New Zealand 1994

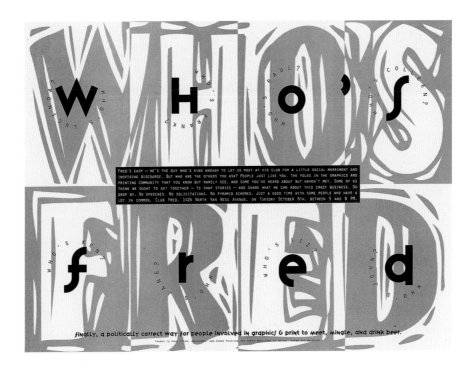

1. AD, D: Charles Shields DF: Shields Design CL: Fresno Graphics Group   USA   1993

2. AD, D: Takaaki Matsumoto DF: Matsumoto Incorporated CL: The Equitable Gallery   USA   1995

JAZZ FROM FINLAND

FROM THE LAND OF THE MIDNIGHT SUN TO THE LAND DOWN UNDER

THE TRIO
TÖYKEÄT

IIRO RANTALA-PIANO EERIK SIIKASAARI-BASS RAMI ESKELINEN-DRUMS

NATIONAL AUSTRALIAN SUMMER TOUR 1994

Thursday 20 & Friday 21 January
Tokyo: Shinjuku Pit Inn   3354 2024

Tuesday 25 January
Victoria: Melbourne
Esplanade Hotel - St. Kilda   534 0211

Thursday 27 & Friday 28 January
Bennetts Lane - City   663 2856

Sunday 30 January
Victoria: Eltham
Montsalvat Jazz Festival   439 7712

Tuesday 1 to Thursday 3 February
New South Wales
Sydney Festival & Carnivale   267 2311

Friday 4 & Saturday 5 February
Queensland
Queensland International Jazz Festival 238 2222

Tuesday 8 February
Kuranda: Rainforest Concert   (070) 937334

Thursday 10 February
New South Wales: Newcastle
Bellair Hotel - Katorah   (049) 57 0253

Friday 11 February
ACT: Canberra
Finnish-Australian Club of Canberra   251 3576

Saturday 12 February
New South Wales
Kiama Jazz Festival   (042) 32 3322

Monday 14 February
Sydney: The Basement - City   251 2797

Tuesday 15 February
Victoria: Melbourne
Esplanade Hotel - St. Kilda   534 0211

Wednesday 16 February
Victoria: Melbourne
Royal Derby Hotel - Fitzroy   417 2321

Thursday 17 February
Mietta's - City   654 2366

Saturday 19 February
Tasmania: Hobart
Tasmanian Jazz Action Society   437 232

Sunday 20 February
South Australia: Adelaide
Jazz Action Society of Sth Aust   277 0096

Monday 21 February
Western Australia: Perth
Hyde Park Hotel - City   328 8898

Tuesday 22 February
Edith Cowan University   370 6832
(Conservatorium Jazz Studies)

Thurs 24 & Sat 26 February
Victoria: Melbourne
Bennetts Lane - City   663 2856

Friday 25 February
Chinta Ria R&B - Carlton   349 2599

"When I first heard the Trio Töykeät play I was totally bowled over....knocked out. I immediately recommended them for work.... I also started hiring them....then they started hiring me!.... Iiro Rantala is one of the best musicians I have ever known..A RARE talent!" - Lew Soloff, trumpetist, New York City, August 1993

"Iiro Rantala is a pianistic sensation who makes the strongest case I know to believe in reincarnation because his pianistic technique and musical sensitivity speak of depth which appear impossible to have been achieved in this lifetime alone...." - Gil Goldstein, pianist, New York City, August 1993

The Trio Töykeät Tour is financially made possible through travel grants from the Finnish Performing Music Promotion Centre (ESEK) and the Foundation for the Promotion of Finnish Music (LUSES)

✈ FINNAIR

The Trio Töykeät and jazz fans from Finland fly Finnair

Hertz

In Australia The Trio Töykeät uses Hertz Rental Car Services

Photo processing by Black & White Production House
Prahran (03) 529 6282

PolyGram
CLASSICS

The Trio Töykeät G'Day Album (Emarcy 518453-2) is available at the concerts and is released through PolyGram Jazz Classics

Presented by: Australia Northern Europe Liaisons
- Henk van Leeuwen phone and fax: 03 510 3662
Poster by Andrew Hoyne Design

AD, D: Andrew Hoyne D: Louisa Gent DF: Andrew Hoyne Design CL: Trio Toykeat Australia 1993

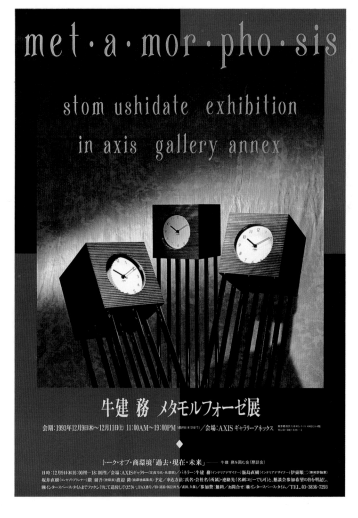

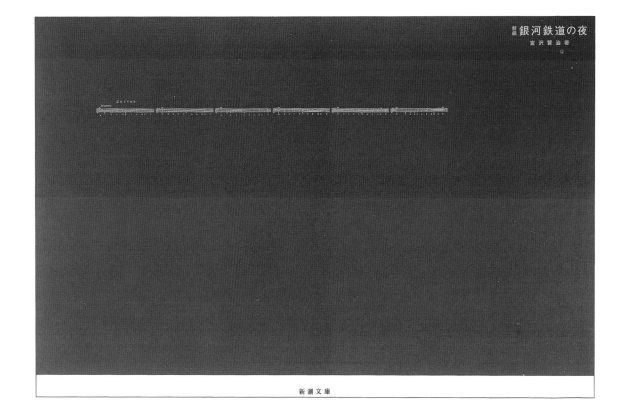

1. CD: Jun Yoshiwara AD, D, DF: Design Kyodai Typographer: Katsunori Aoki I: Gugi Akiyama CL: Jun & Yoko Yoshiwara   Japan   1992

2. AD, D: Norio Nakamura CL: Shinchosha   Japan   1993

1. CD, AD, D: Richard Poulin DF: Richard Poulin Design Group Inc. CL: The Asia Society   USA   1990

2. CD, AD, D, I: Lanny Sommese DF: Sommese Design CL: Penn State Graphic Design Dept.   USA   1993

CD, AD: Koji Mizutani D, DF: Mizutani Studio PH: Takahisa Ide   Japan   1990

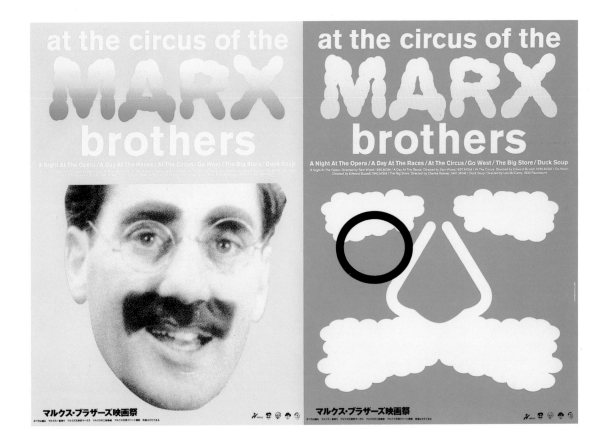

1. AD, D: Tycoon Graphics CL: Nippon Helard Films   Japan   1993

2. AD, D, I: Simon Sernec CL: Nina & Tatiana Mole   Slovenia   1994

AD, D: Lau Siu Hong D: Veronica Cheung Lai Sheung PH: C K Wong DF: Kan Tai-Keung Design & Associates Ltd. CL: Zuni Icosahedron Hong Kong 1994

PARCO

Design by Contemporary Production

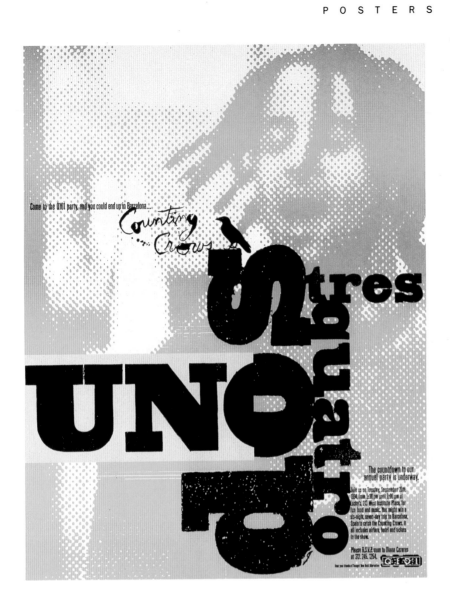

the salvation of **iggy scrooge**

1. AD, D, I: Daniel Smith / Joseph Cachero PH: Chris Bennion DF: NBBJ Graphic Design CL: The Empty Space Theatre   USA   1994

2. CD: Dave Crider D: Art Chantry I: Edwin Judah Fotheringham DF: Art Chantry Design CL: Estrus   USA   1994

1. D, I: Rian Hughes DF: Device CL: Font Shop (Berlin) UK 1994

2. CD: Takahiro Suzuki AD, D: Fukushi Okubo CL: Tower Records Inc. Japan 1994

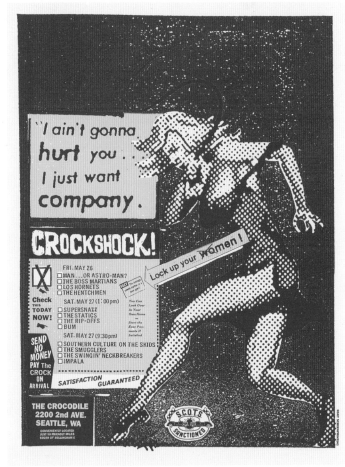

1. D: Art Chantry DF: Art Chantry Design CL: Moe's Mo'Rockin' Cafe   USA   1995

2. D: Art Chantry DF: Art Chantry Design CL: Crocodile Cafe   USA   1995

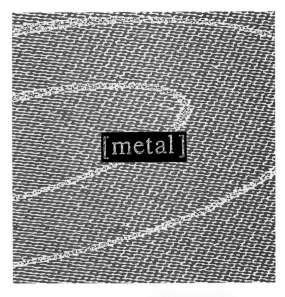

CD, AD, D: Peat Jariya D: Gerakis DF: Peat Jariya Design / [METAL] CL: [METAL] Studio Corp. USA 1992 Brochure

M

CD, AD, D, I: Paul West / Paula Benson PH: Spiros DF: Form CL: Epic Records / 2wo Third3 UK 1994 Brochure

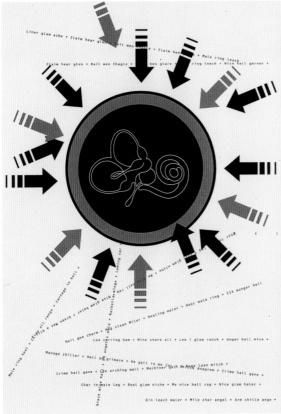

My name is Lee. Ref No: L 25 03 71.
To whom it may concern. Let me begin
this fact-find with a physical
description as I think it is of some
relevance here. I'm a 22 year old
arien possessing of a youthful boyish
physique which compliments my height
of 5'8½". I am smooth and very firm
with pleasing muscle definition.
I have dark blue eyes and short dark
hair. Visual stimulation is important
to me sexually. I get off on
giving and receiving subtle erog-
enous sensation and of course more
full blooded physical passion. As a
graduate of communication studies I
enjoy a promising career as a singer
in the entertainment sector.
I conduct a very disciplined and
flexible workout and have an
income which draws me to a comfort-
able standard of living. My general
interests include cinema, couture,
croquet and - saving - oh I hate the
phrase but a rock and roll lifestyle.
I would love to travel more but am re
the-city and am firmly established
in London. Quality of life is
important to me and I believe in
continually scaling opportunities for
self-expression and serious pleasure.
Call or write if you would like to
get together. Once more my name is
Lee. Ref No: L 25 03 71. Goodbye.

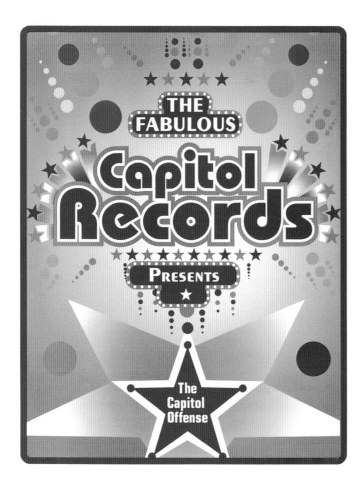

1. CD: Jeff Fey AD, D, I: George Estrada DF: Modern Dog CL: Capital Records   USA   1994   Magazine cover

2. CD: Jeff Fey AD, D: Michael Strassburger DF: Modern Dog CL: Capitol Offense   USA   1994   Magazine cover

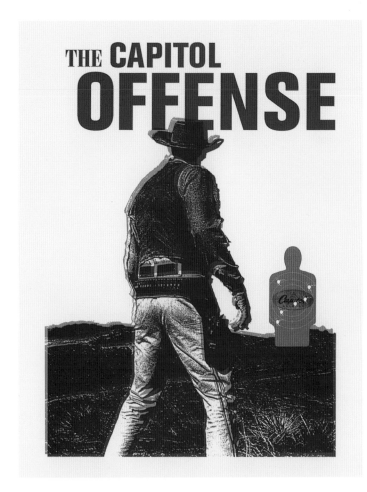

1. CD: Jeff Fey AD, D: Robynne Raye DF: Modern Dog CL: Capitol Records   USA   1994   Magazine cover

2. CD: Jeff Fey AD, D: Robynne Raye DF: Modern Dog CL: Capitol Records   USA   1994   Magazine cover

"There is nothing training cannot do.
Nothing is above its reach" Mark Twain

There is nothing training cannot do. Nothing is above its reach

APM Training Institute

Providing Skills, Experience and Opportunities

This prospectus outlines how APM Training Institute can provide you with the skills, experience and opportunity to boost your career. It details the courses that are available in 1995, as well as information on the faculty and resources of APM Training Institute.

"Our congratulations to APM Training Institute for their commitment to high quality, leading edge marketing education. We look forward to continuing our strong relationship with you and your students" Bill Leigh (FAMI) Manager Australian Marketing Institute

Table of contents:

CD, AD, D: Mark Denning DF: Mark Denning Graphics Pty Ltd. CL: APM Training Institute   Australia 1995 Brochure

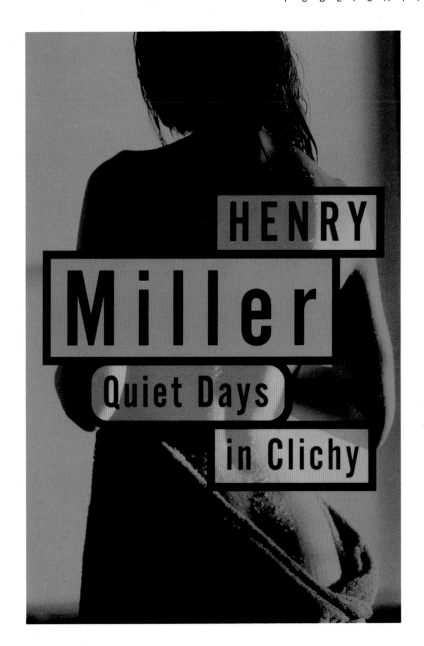

1. **AD, D:** John Gall **PH:** Barnaby Hall **DF:** In-House **CL:** Grove/Atlantic Inc.   USA   1994   Book cover

2. **AD, D:** Yoshinari Hisazumi **PH:** Katsutoshi Hatsuzawa **DF:** Hisazumi Design Room **CL:** The Mainichi Newspapers   Japan   1994   Magazine cover

CD, AD, D: Jacques Koeweiden / Paul Postma D: Eric Hesen PH: Jaap Stahlie DF: Koeweiden Postma Associates CL: Swets & Zeitlinger Publishers Netherlands 1992-95 Brochures

CD, AD, D: Jacques Koeweiden / Paul Postma D: Eric Hesen PH: Jaap Stahlie DF: Koeweiden Postma Associates CL: Swets & Zeitlinger Publishers   Netherlands   1992-95   Brochures

CD, D: Ciaran Ogaora D: Stoffel Den Drijver PH: Folkert Helmus / Jaap V. Dbeukel DF: Proforma Association for Designers and Consultants CL: Lantaren/Venster Netherlands
1994-95 Magazine covers

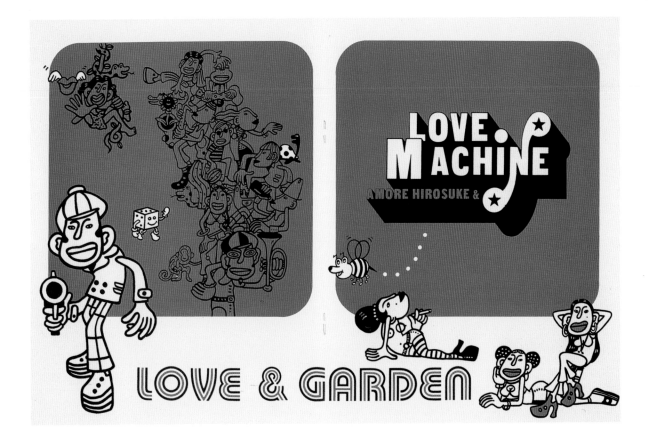

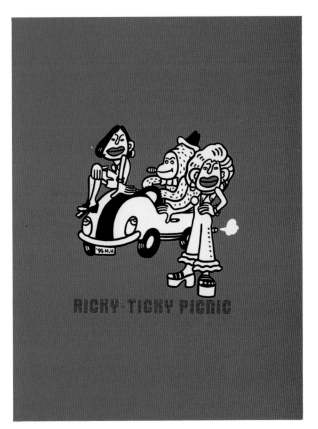

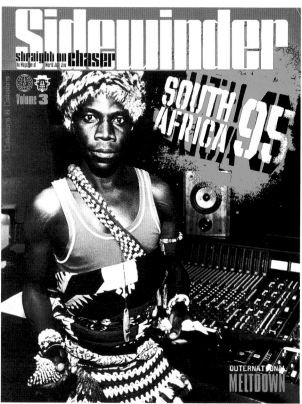

1. CD, AD, D: Swifty PH: Pav Modelski DF: Swifty Typografix CL: Straight No Chaser UK 1994 Magazine cover

2. CD, AD, D: Swifty PH: Peter Williams DF: Swifty Typografix CL: Straight No Chaser UK 1994 Magazine cover

3. CD, AD, D: Swifty PH: Peter Williams DF: Swifty Typografix CL: Straight No Chaser UK 1995 Magazine cover

4. CD, AD, D: Swifty DF: Swifty Typografix CL: Gilles Peterson UK 1994 Magazine cover

1. CD, AD, D: Swifty PH: Chris Clunn DF: Swifty Typografix CL: Straight No Chaser   UK   1995   Magazine page

2. CD, AD, D: Swifty PH: Peter Williams DF: Swifty Typografix CL: Straight No Chaser   UK   1995   Magazine page

3. CD, AD, D: Swifty PH: Liz Johnson-Arthur DF: Swifty Typografix CL: Straight No Chaser   UK   1995   Magazine page

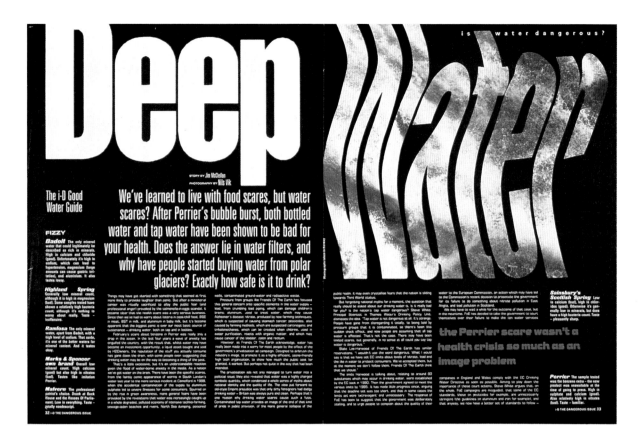

1. CD, AD, D, DF: Stephen Male PH: Jean Baptiste Mondino CL: I-D Magazine UK 1990 Magazine page

2. CD, AD, D, DF: Stephen Male CL: Post Magazine UK 1989 Magazine page

Coming To Your Planet Soon

2

2049
Arctic – Arctic and Siberian Tundra may have warmed 6-8 degrees centigrade, melting and releasing stored methane, a greenhouse gas twenty times as powerful, molecule-for-molecule, as carbon dioxide.

2050
Climate change due to the greenhouse effect may have raised the strength of hurricanes by 40-50%, and winds that reach 280 kph in the 1980's will be reaching 350 kph.

2060
All forests in Africa, Latin America, Asia, North America and Pacific developed countries will have been lost, if clearance continues at 1980s levels as a function of population growth. Carbon release from burning these forest will be 375 billion tonnes. This is more than the total fossil fuel release up to 1988.

2070
Pacific – the islands of Tuvalu and Kiribati in the Pacific Maldives are expected to be submerged by a sea level rise of two metres. The 1988 population of the Maldives was 177,000. In Bangladesh, 9% of the population (10

million people) live in the area that would be inundated by a 3m sea level rise

2100
The world population is projected to reach 10.1 billion
Americas – the rise in sea levels due to the greenhouse effect is projected to have cost US$ 111 billion and to have taken 18,000 square kilometres of land, in the United States
All accessible tropical forests in Latin America will have been destroyed, if rates increase exponentially from 1980, from 11m Ha to 15m Ha a year.

2165
According to a model produced by the US EPA in 1988 chlorine pollution responsible for ozone depletion in the stratosphere, will return towards natural levels, given a 100% reduction in CFCs in 1988. 100% compliance by all nations, a freeze on substances such as methyl chloroform and limits on others

1001989
A million years from 1989 nuclear waste sites in the 1980's will be safe. They will have had to survive sea level change and ten ice ages

1

the time of the rainbow warriors

4

intermediate level nuclear waste, and 770,000 cubic metres of low level waste. The amount of high level waste will be 3,335 cubic metres, costing £498,900 per cubic metre to dispose of. The overall cost will be £4.3 billion soon after 2000
Space – there will be so much 'space junk' circulating the earth – thousands of pieces of debris accumulating from satellites and rockets in orbit – that there is a 1 in 20 probability of a satellite being disabled by an object the size of a coin, every year.
Europe – As a result of acid rain soil acidification may now affect 60-70% of soils in Europe, seven times the level affected in 1987

2010
USA – the US department of energy expects to have had to spend US$ 128 billion at 1989 rates on safety improvements at nuclear plants.
Worldwide – chlorine pollution of the stratosphere will have trebled over 1989 levels, even if a ban on ozone depleting CFCs is in place by 2000
Tropics – all tropical forest in Sri Lanka, Costa Rica, Côte d'Ivoire, Nigeria and El Salvador will be lost if deforestation proceeds at 1980s rates.

2021
Europe – the majority of soils in Europe will be nitrogen saturated if pollution deposition rates are not reduced below critical loads, that is by 60-90% from 1980 levels. This will lead to severe deforestation

2025
The world population is projected to reach 8.2 billion

2026
Europe – It is estimated that in the European

Community 1,090 people will have died from cancers and other sickness induced by the Chernobyl accident in 1986. It is also estimated that 30,000 people will have died from cancer worldwide as a result of the accident half in the USSR, including 100 new leukaemia deaths

2028
Africa – the African elephant population is forecast to have dwindled from 750,000 in 1988 to 2,000-12,000

2030
Greenhouse gas concentrations may have effectively doubled over pre-industrial times and the mean global temperature may have risen 2-3 degrees centigrade. This means creating a 4-6 degree centigrade rise in Minneapolis and a consequent 100-500 km retreat of forest and advance of prairie vegetation for each degree. Average winter temperatures in the Arctic may rise as much as 8-10 degrees centigrade. Forests are likely to occur over a 400-600 km wide belt across the USA. A 1.3-4.5 degree centigrade rise will be the hottest earth temperature for 125,000 years. An increase of 3 degrees might release 224-380 billion tonnes and 3.8 degree rise might release 600 billion tonnes of carbon from soils, more than a century's release from burning fossil fuel at 1980's rates. Sea levels may have risen 0.2 - 2 metres, causing up to 300,000 islanders in the south Pacific and Indian Oceans to abandon their homes. Even if annual emission cuts were introduced in 1988, stopping the growth in additional man-made warming by 2000, the earth will still be 1 degree centigrade warmer by 2030-33. That is warmer than it has been for 6,200 years. Worldwide vehicle registrations are projected to exceed 1 billion. This is double the late 1980's level, when carbon monoxide from cars was indirectly responsible for 20-40% of global warming

A chronology of recent environmental disasters...

6

nuclear submarine sinks 500 kilometres off Norway. 42 sailors die. Its two reactors contain liquid metal coolants thought to include lead and bismuth. It is the eighth nuclear submarine to be lost. It has two nuclear torpedoes on board.
April **UK** – Britain's electricity industry now emits 233 million tonnes of carbon dioxide, 869,000 tonnes of oxides of nitrogen, gases causing the greenhouse effect and 2.8 million tonnes of sulphur dioxide, the principle cause of acid rain, each year.
May 12 **Worldwide** – the total toxicity of metals dumped around the world each year exceed that of all radioactive chemicals put together. Cadmium, mercury, arsenic and other toxic metals are entering the food chain and probably causing long term epidemics of

cancer and reproductive disorders. The depositions worldwide total at least 7 million tonnes.
May. **Alaska** – 15 million sea birds, waders and waterfowl are expected to arrive in southern central Alaska, the area including Prince William Sound, which is contaminated with oil from the Valdez spill.
May **USA** – the cost of cleaning up toxic waste dumps in the USA will be US $100 billion, more than the entire profits of the top 'Fortune 500' US companies. Up to 425,000 hazardous waste sites exist in the USA.
May. **Ohio, USA** – the Feed Materials Production Centre in Ohio, a plant making uranium for nuclear weapons, has discharged six times the amount of radioactive dust into the environment than has previously been admitted.

5

Coming To Your Planet Soon

As of 1990 there are now nearly 400 nuclear reactors in operation. From past experience it is expected that a serious accident with a nuclear reactor will occur every 1500 years of reactor operation. This means an accident every 4 years.

1994
USA – 253 plant species native to the United States and living in 1989 may be extinct due to habitat loss.

1999
High-level radioactive waste from the world's nuclear reactors (operating or being built in 1988) will top 150,000 million curies.

2000
The world population is projected to reach 6.1 billion, an increase of a billion in 20 years.
China plans to have a refrigerator in each household. As of 1989 it was planned that these several hundred million refrigerators would use 132 million kilogrammes of hard CFC11 and CFC12, the type most damaging to the ozone layer.
UK – Britain is due to have 60,000 cubic metres of

CD, AD, DF: Stephen Male   D: Neil Edwards   CL: Greenpeace   UK   1989   Brochure pages

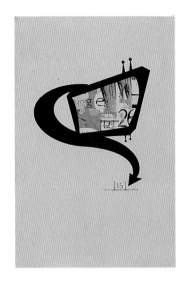

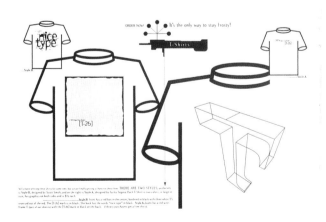

CD, AD, D: Carlos Segura DF: Segura Inc. CL: [T-26] USA 1995 Brochure

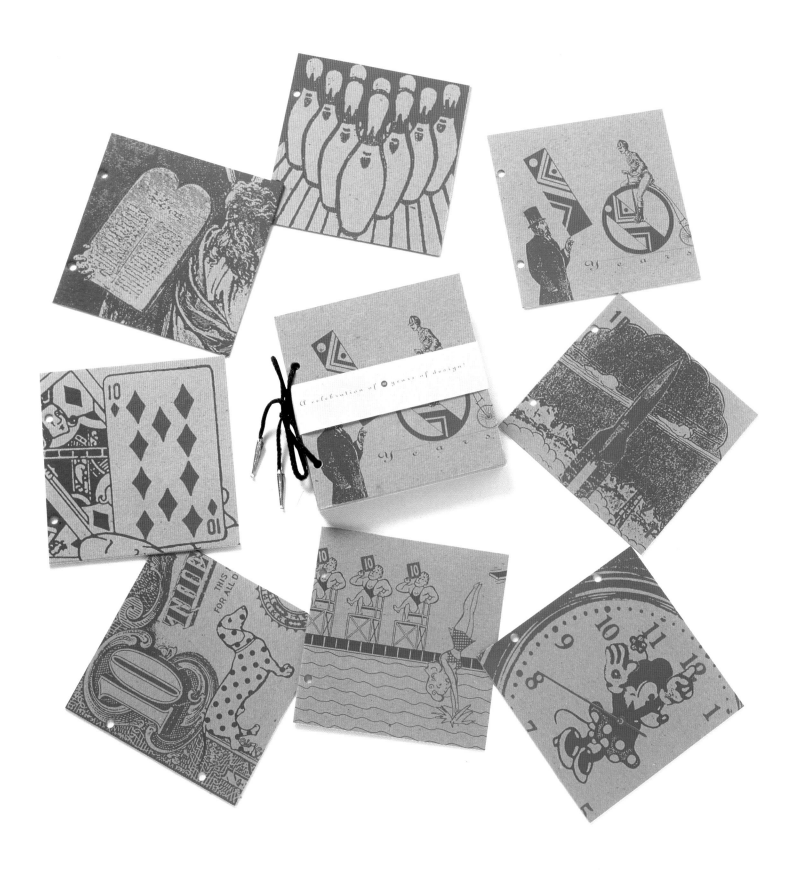

CD, AD, D: Rick Vaughn DF, CL: Vaughn Wedeen Creative   USA   1992   Brochure

CD: Sharon Chandler AD, D, I: Michael Strassburger D, I: Robynne Raye / Vittorio Costarella / George Estrada DF: Modern Dog CL: Gilbert Paper Company   USA 1995 Brochure

MB

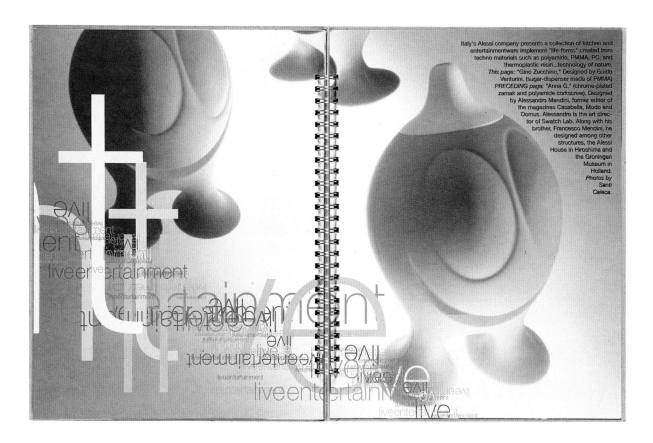

Italy's Alessi company presents a collection of kitchen and entertainmentware implement "life-forms" created from techno materials such as polyamide, PMMA, PC, and thermoplastic resin...technology of nature. *This page:* "Gino Zucchino," Designed by Guido Venturini. (sugar-dispenser made of PMMA) *PRECEDING page:* "Anna G." (chrome-plated zamak and polyamide corkscrew). Designed by Alessandro Mendini, former editor of the magazines Casabella, Modo and Domus. Alessandro is the art director of Swatch Lab. Along with his brother, Francesco Mendini, he designed among other structures, the Alessi House in Hiroshima and the Groningen Museum in Holland. *Photos by Santi Caleca.*

the mÂp interview:
Hideto Fusé

Japan's best-selling author and foremost neuroscientist talks with us about technology, nature, art and the human brain

CD, AD, D: Robert Bergman-Ungar DF: Bergman-Ungar Associates CL: MÂP USA 1994 Magazine pages

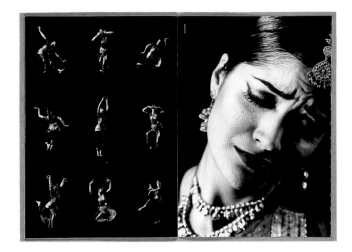

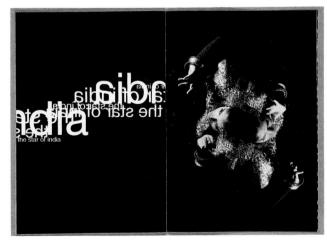

CD, AD, D: Robert Bergman-Ungar   DF: Bergman-Ungar Associates   CL: MAP   USA   1994   Magazine pages

MB

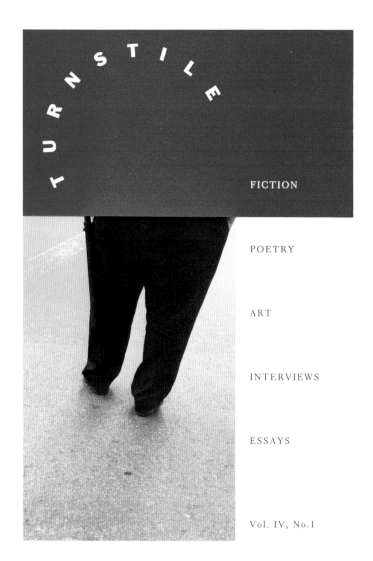

TURNSTILE

FICTION

POETRY

ART

INTERVIEWS

ESSAYS

Vol. IV, No.1

1. AD, D, PH: John Gall **DF:** John Gall Graphic Design **CL:** Turnstile USA 1993 **Book cover**

M
V

2. D: John Gall **PH:** Elliot Erwitt **DF:** John Gall Graphic Design **CL:** St. Martin's Press USA 1994 **Book cover**

D: Art Chantry DF: Art Chantry Design CL: Nemzoff/Roth Touring Artists   USA 1995 Brochure

AD, D: Tycoon Graphics I: Hiro Sugiyama / Ichiro Tanida CL: Nippon Herald Films Japan 1994 Brochure

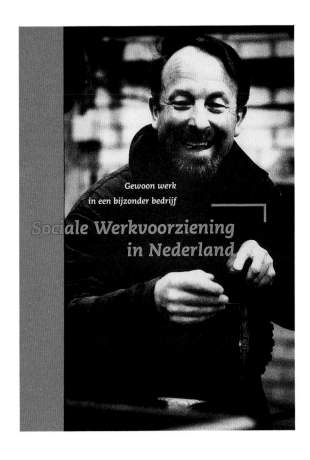

Gewoon werk
in een bijzonder bedrijf

Sociale Werkvoorziening
in Nederland

12 | Opleiding

SW-bedrijven willen hun werknemers zo goed mogelijk arbeidsgeschikt maken. Scholing en opleiding zijn daarbij heel belangrijk. U kunt zelf aangeven wat u wilt. Een heel nieuw vak leren bijvoorbeeld. Of een praktijkcursus volgen om uw vakbekwaamheid als drukker of lasser te vergroten. Een landelijk erkend diploma halen kan ook. SW-bedrijven werken daartoe samen met het Leerlingwezen en met het Landelijk Bureau Arbeidsvoorziening. Veel opleidingen en trainingen vinden binnen het SW-bedrijf plaats. Soms gaat u naar een streekschool of een andere locatie buiten het SW-bedrijf. In al die gevallen wordt uw salaris gewoon doorbetaald.

Door te werken en te leren tegelijk krijgt u meer kansen op de arbeidsmarkt. Sommige SW-medewerkers kunnen, als ze dat willen, na enkele jaren ergens anders gaan werken. Bij bedrijven, bij instellingen of bij de overheid.

Teus Verhoef, Jan van Wijk en Wim Kreuers zijn werkzaam in de groenvoorziening. Zij volgen hier met veel enthousiasme een interne cursus boomzaaien onder leiding van een docent van een gerenommeerd instituut.

Wilt u meer weten? Neemt u dan contact op met het SW-bedrijf bij u in de buurt. Voor algemene informatie kunt u terecht bij het NOSW (Nationaal Overlegorgaan Sociale Werkvoorziening).

Het adres is
NOSW
Karel Doormanlaan 155   Telefoon (070) 336 00 62
2283 AL Rijswijk   Fax (070) 336 05 84

Colofon
Uitgave van het Nationaal Overlegorgaan
Sociale Werkvoorziening

Tekst
Heleen van Antwerpen (NOSW)

Fotografie
Maarten Laupman
Foto's zijn gemaakt bij de Alblasserwaard
en de Vijfheerenlanden te Gorinchem

Vormgeving
Proforma ontwerp & advies bNO

Drukkerij
CombiWerk Delft

Mei 1995

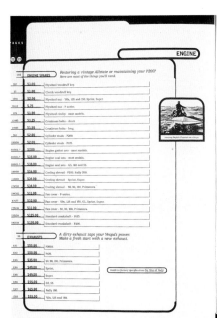

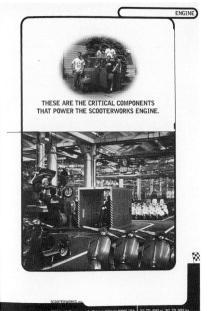

THESE ARE THE CRITICAL COMPONENTS
THAT POWER THE SCOOTERWORKS ENGINE.

5709 North Ravenswood. Chicago, Illinois 60660. 312. 271.4242 tel. 312. 271. 5012 fax

Scooter WORKS USA

Vespa

The 38th Annual
Goddard Memorial Dinner

The 38th Annual
Goddard Memorial Dinner

Awards and Scholarships
March 24, 1995

Agenda

Introduction of
Distinguished Guests
James F. Kukowski

Invocation
Chaplain Major General
Donald J. Harlin,
Chief of Air Force
Chaplains

Presentation of Colors
Joint Armed Forces Color
Guard

Welcoming Remarks
Thomas H. Brownell
President,
National Space Club

Keynote Speaker
Ray Bradbury

Presentation of National
Space Club Awards

The Dr. Robert H. Goddard
Historical Essay Award

The Olin E. Teague
Memorial Scholarship

The Dr. Robert H. Goddard
Scholarship

The Dr. Hugh L. Dryden
Memorial Science
Fellowship

The Dr. George M. Low
Memorial Engineering
Fellowship

The James E. Webb
Memorial Space
Administration Fellowship

The National Space Club
Space Educator Award

The Eagle Manned Mission
Success Award

The Astronautics Engineer
Award

The National Space Club
Science Award

The Nelson P. Jackson
Aerospace Award

Presentation of the 1995
Dr. Robert H. Goddard
Memorial Trophy

Closing Remarks

Dancing

Music
Military, by the United
States Air Force Band;
during and after dinner,
by the Starlite Orchestra

The Nelson P. Jackson
Aerospace Award

1995 Recipient
The Clementine I
Spacecraft Mission
Management Team

Citation for innovative
spacecraft design, deve-
lopment and operations,
and the production of
meaningful scientific data
that was used to build the
most comprehensive,
multispectral geologic
lunar map to date.

The recipient of the award
is selected annually by the
National Space Club from
the aerospace industry; the
selected firm having been
responsible during the
preceding year for an outstanding contribution to the
missile, aircraft and space
field. The award is a
memorial to the late Nelson
P. (Pete) Jackson, one of
the founders and past
president of the National
Space Club.

Award Committee

Non-Voting Chairman:
Bill Witt
Lockheed Missiles & Space
Company

Lt. Gen. James A.
Abrahamson
USAF (Ret.)
Oracle Corporation

James R. Asker
Aviation Week & Space
Technology

Rear Adm. Thomas C.
Betterton
USN (Ret.)

Hugh Downs
National Space Institute

Dr. Robert A. Frosch
Harvard University

The Honorable Harrison
H. Schmitt
Aerospace Consultant

The Dr. Robert H. Goddard
Memorial Trophy

1995 Recipient
Gen. Thomas S. Moorman, Jr.
United States Air Force

Citation: Through numerous
national space leadership
positions, he exhibited
extraordinary leadership,
vision and commitment to
advancing the United
States' military, civil and
commercial space pro-
grams and built a national
consensus for strength-
ening the world's premier
space-faring nation.

The recipient of the
award is selected annually
for great achievement in
advancing space flight
programs contributing to
United States leadership in
astronautics. The trophy,
the premier award of the
National Space Club, was
established in 1958 and
is presented each year at
the Goddard Memorial
Dinner. The permanent
trophy is a half-life-size
bust of Dr. Goddard,
sculpted in bronze and
mounted on a marble base.

Award Committee

The Board of Governors
of the National Space Club,
voting by secret ballot

CD: Mary Jo Ondrejka AD, D: Ramona Hutko PH: NASA DF: Computer Sciences Corporation, Presentations and Publications Department CL: National Space Club

USA 1995 Brochure

I have been involved in the development of solid state transducers for a number of years, seeking alternatives to the use of piezo in recording. There is no need here to go into the disadvantages and shortcomings of piezo-electric pickups - they are well enough known to professional musicians.

I made a significant advance in 1985 with the construction of a bridge pick-up for the double-bass based on electrostatic principles. The worldwide success of this pick-up indicated that I was proceeding along the right lines.

But I personally always considered this as merely a first - even wrongheaded - step. Despite the electrostatic transducer's linear response with regard to the kind of large amplitudes characteristic of the sounding board of a piano or the belly of a double-bass, it is really not ideal. The next task was clear : to find the "physically perfect soundless transducer". Soundless because even in the back row we want to hear the pianist and only the pianist - not the pick-up.

I was determined that even the harshest piano chord should be within the dynamic range of my sought-after transducer, and that the resulting reproduction had to be as pure and faithful to the heaviest double-bass rhythms as to the fieriness of the flamenco guitar.

It turned out that only one electrodynamic transducer could meet such stringent requirements. Years of further research and development were required to bring the original concept to the point where it could be applied generally to all acoustic instruments.

I present the results of all this work to you in this brochure, not without a certain pride, in the conviction that this new generation of transducers will open a whole new world of acoustic possibility to the discerning user.

If you get the feeling during a performance that your instrument, equipped with the SCHERTLER AUDIO TRANSDUCER, sounds entirely "acoustic", just as if you were sitting in your living-room at home, then I will feel my efforts have been worthwhile - just precisely in that I have added nothing at all to your sound.

Regards,

and the SCHERTLER AUDIO TRANSDUCERS team

The electrodynamic solid state transducer has been developed by SCHERTLER AUDIO TRANSDUCERS and patented worldwide.

The advantages of this transducer are best illustrated by a comparison with the good old record-player. The best cartridges (in conjunction with the rest of the system of course) guarantee ideal sound reproduction. The unconstrained motion of the needle as it traces the shape of the groove plus the accurate conversion of this motion into voltage ensure an uncoloured audio reproduction.

WHAT MAKES THE SCHERTLER AUDIO TRANSDUCER UNIQUE

The same holds for the electrodynamic transducer. In this case the "MOVING COIL" is attached to the instrument via a spring connector and moves in a decoupled magnetic field. The magnet stays still while the coil vibrates with the instrument, causing the well-known voltage differential. The decoupling of the magnet is achieved by means of springs and damping linkages, disposed according to Butterworth's Second Law, resulting in an (at least theoretically) completely linear frequency response. In practice it's possible to achieve the linearity of a studio mike. You might then want to turn your attention to the frequency response of your loudspeakers ...

Connecting up the SCHERTLER could not be simpler. Power supplies, DI-boxes, preamps - forget them. Thanks to low impedance and balanced design, each mixing unit receives the signal directly from the transducer or via a microphone cable, just as from a mike, with no hum, compatibility problems or cable leakage. Try getting the same from a piezo pickup!

All transducer models are mounted on the body of the instrument. The sensors within the casing of the transducer are free to ensure the immediate transmission of the vibration from the instrument to the coil. The mount itself can be detached from the instrument without damaging the surface.

Each transducer is supplied in a handy solid wooden case together with all accessories. A detailed instruction booklet is included - we aim to ensure satisfaction from the word go.

The highest quality assurance standards during the production process each transducer is tested six times - mean that we have no hesitation in offering a full 2-year guarantee for every part of the system.

CD, AD: Stefan Sagmeister D: Eric Zim PH: Tom Schierlitz DF: Sagmeister Inc. CL: Stephan Schertler Switzerland 1994 Brochure

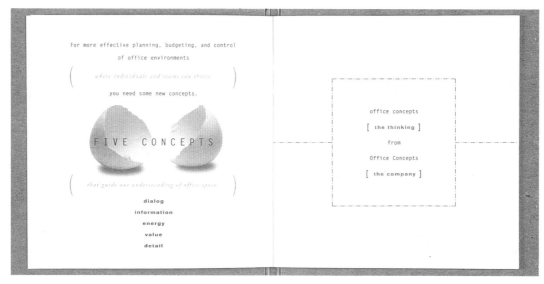

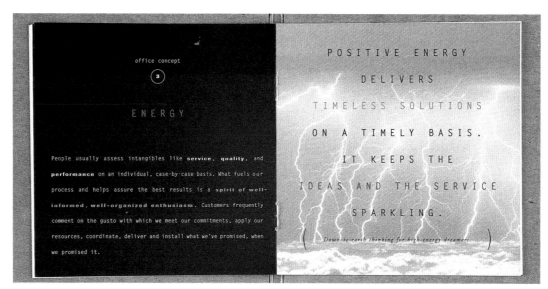

CD, AD: Mark Oldach AD, D: Don Emery I: Mary Flock DF: Mark Oldach Design CL: Office Concepts   USA   1995   Brochure

As intricate as a leaf's water transportation system,

M.U.D.'s network services close to 300,000 customers.

The leaves of plants and trees break down water into the gas, oxygen, which is then released into the atmosphere.

CD, AD, D: Carter Weitz PH: Jim Krantz DF: Bailey Lauerman & Associates CL: Metropolitan Utilities District USA 1992 Brochure

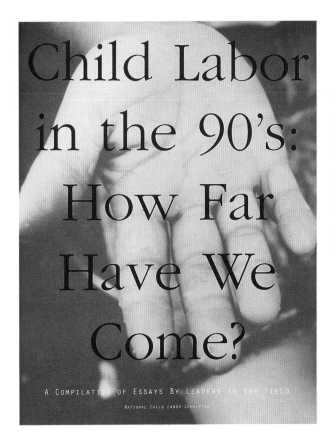

Child Labor in the 90's: How Far Have We Come?

A COMPILATION OF ESSAYS BY LEADERS IN THE FIELD

NATIONAL CHILD LABOR COMMITTEE

THE SCOURGE OF CHILD LABOR IN AMERICA: BACK TO THE FUTURE

BILL GOOLD
LEGISLATIVE DIRECTOR AND PRESS SECRETARY TO
U.S. REPRESENTATIVE GEORGE E. BROWN, JR.

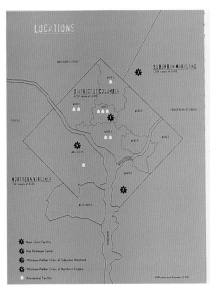

LOCATIONS

1992 RESOURCES

VOLUNTEERS »1,862 active volunteers«
»Dollar value of contributed work—$7,508,000«

STAFF »134 full-time staff«

BUDGET »Annual budget of $10.2 million«

DEVELOPMENT »AIDSWalk—22,000 walkers raised over $1 million« »Community Campaigns—raised $1.4 million from United Way, Combined Federal Campaign and DC One Fund« »Special Events«

ADVOCACY
SHELTER
CONCERN
CARE
VIGILANCE
Whitman-Walker Clinic, Inc.
RESEARCH
1992 Annual Report
NOURISHMENT
HEALING
NURSING
GRIEF
OUTREACH
COMFORT
EDUCATION
ESSENTIALS.

1. AD, D: Steven Brower PH: Lewis Wicks Hine / Nancy Buirski DF: Steven Brower Design CL: National Child Labor Committee USA 1995 Brochure

MB

2. AD, D: Samuel G. Shelton / Jeffrey Fabian / Amy Gustincic PH: Linda Bartlett / Prayoon Charoennum / Michael Keating / Barbara Kinney / Barry Myers / Kyle Samperton
DF: KINETIK Communication Graphics, Inc. CL: Whitman-Walker Clinic, Inc. USA 1994 Brochure

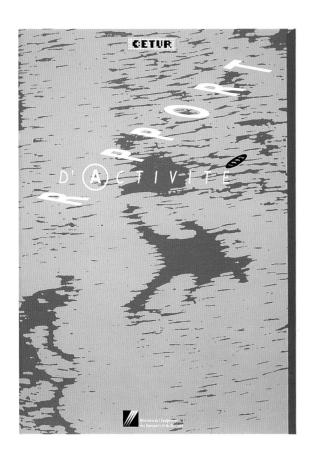

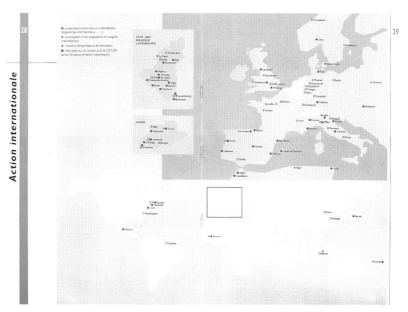

EDUCATION
AND EMPLOYMENT

*The American Express Foundation made
over 70 grants in 1993 and 1994 to improve
New York City public schools.*

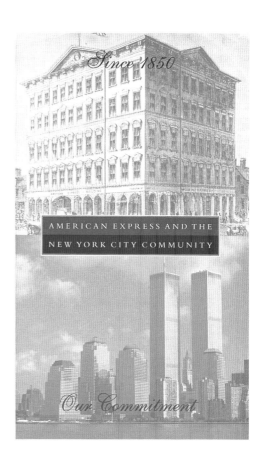

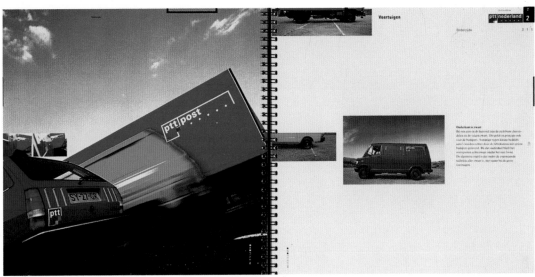

CD: Michel De Boer AD: Henri Ritzen D: Studio Dumbar Staff PH: Victor Nieuwenhuis / Lex Van Pieterson I: Berry Van Gerwen DF: Studio Dumbar CL: Royal Dutch PTT
Netherlands 1989 Manual

SAN FRANCISCO A rt INSTITUTE

classes

Drawing
Figure Drawing
Painting
Advanced Painting Workshop
Mixed Media Painting
Watercolor
Black & White Photography
Color Photography
Pinhole and Plastic Photography
Voice & Vision
Printmaking
Fine Art Filmmaking
Figure Sculpture in Clay
Mold Making and Casting

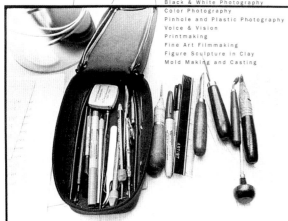

Extension
education

95 summer

Saturday and Evening Classes

Classes
Drawing
Figure Drawing
Painting
Advanced Painting Workshop
Mixed Media Painting
Black and White Photography
Color Photography
Low-Tech Lighting Solutions
Thursday Evening Critique
Printmaking
Fine Art Filmmaking
Figure Sculpture in Clay
Metal Sculpture

Education

EXTENSION

Saturday and Evening Classes

Winter

**San Francisco
Art Institute**

CD: Pahi Quill AD, D: Raul Cabra D: Martin Venezky DF: Cabra Diseño CL: San Francisco Art Institute   USA   1994   Pamphlet covers

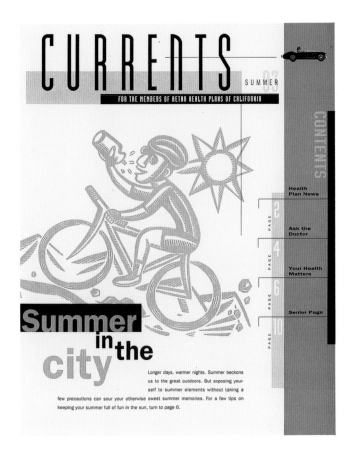

CURRENTS
SUMMER

FOR THE MEMBERS OF AETNA HEALTH PLANS OF CALIFORNIA

Summer
in the
city

Longer days, warmer nights. Summer beckons us to the great outdoors. But exposing yourself to summer elements without taking a few precautions can sour your otherwise sweet summer memories. For a few tips on keeping your summer full of fun in the sun, turn to page 6.

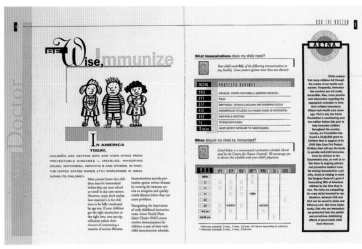

CURRENTS
SPRING

FOR THE MEMBERS OF AETNA HEALTH PLANS OF CALIFORNIA

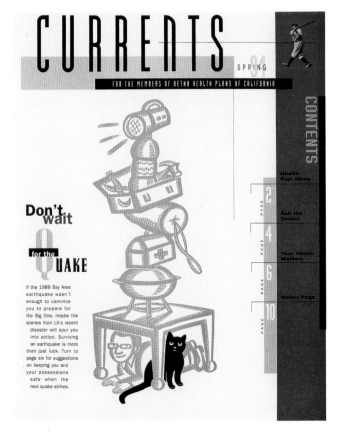

Don't
wait
for the
QUAKE

If the 1989 Bay Area earthquake wasn't enough to convince you to prepare for the Big One, maybe the scenes from LA's recent disaster will spur you into action. Surviving an earthquake is more than just luck. Turn to page six for suggestions on keeping you and your possessions safe when the next quake strikes.

CD: Grace Hammerstrom   AD, D: Raul Cabra   D: Tin-Tin Blackwell   I: Thorina Rose   DF: Cabra Diseño   CL: Aetna Health Insurance   USA   1993-95   Newsletters

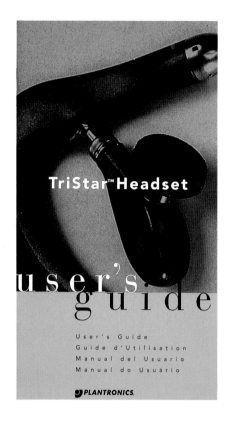

TriStar™ Headset

user's
guide

User's Guide
Guide d'Utilisation
Manual del Usuario
Manual do Usuário

PLANTRONICS.

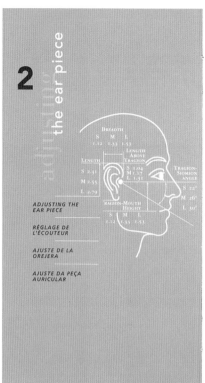

2

adjusting
the ear piece

ADJUSTING THE
EAR PIECE

RÉGLAGE DE
L'ÉCOUTEUR

AJUSTE DE LA
OREJERA

AJUSTE DA PEÇA
AURICULAR

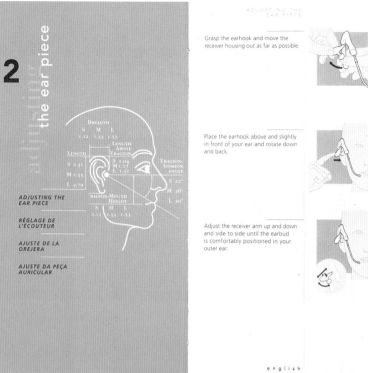

ADJUSTING THE
EAR PIECE

Grasp the earhook and move the
receiver housing out as far as possible.

Place the earhook above and slightly
in front of your ear and rotate down
and back.

Adjust the receiver arm up and down
and side to side until the earbud
is comfortably positioned in your
outer ear.

english

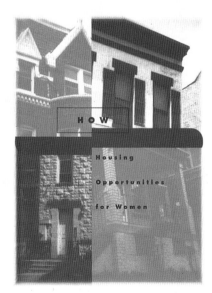

HOW

Housing

Opportunities

for Women

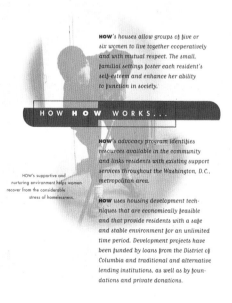

HOW's houses allow groups of five or
six women to live together cooperatively
and with mutual respect. The small,
familial settings foster each resident's
self-esteem and enhance her ability
to function in society.

HOW HOW WORKS...

HOW's supportive and
nurturing environment helps women
recover from the considerable
stress of homelessness.

HOW's advocacy program identifies
resources available in the community
and links residents with existing support
services throughout the Washington, D.C.,
metropolitan area.

HOW uses housing development techniques that are economically feasible
and that provide residents with a safe
and stable environment for an unlimited
time period. Development projects have
been funded by loans from the District of
Columbia and traditional and alternative
lending institutions, as well as by foun-
dations and private donations.

1. CD: Daniel Aescnbacher AD, D: Raul Cabra D: Maxine Ressler I: Studio Q' DF: Cabra Diseño CL: Plantronics USA 1995 User guide

2. AD: Samuel G. Shelton / Jeffrey Fabian D: Amy Gustincic PH: Peter B. Vance DF: KINETIK Communication Graphics, Inc. CL: Housing Opportunities for Women
USA 1995 Brochure

L'ospedale rappresenta oggi una delle realtà più difficili e complesse da governare. Deve infatti assolvere la sua missione, l'assistenza e la cura del malato, affrontando e risolvendo contemporaneamente tutti i problemi propri di una grande organizzazione: la gestione amministrativa, la gestione delle risorse umane e strumentali, anche di tipo molto sofisticato, l'efficace circolazione delle informazioni, le attività di ricerca, come anche tutti gli aspetti legati alla vita quotidiana di una comunità di centinaia o migliaia di persone. ¶ Oltre ad una gestione efficiente delle risorse, deve svolgere un'azione di pianificazione e programmazione che sappia guardare lontano, senza mai perdere di vista i bisogni e i diritti del malato. ¶ Il nuovo quadro normativo rafforza oggi questi difficili impegni ed obiettivi, definendo per l'ospedale nuovi e importanti strumenti operativi e modalità organizzative. ¶ L'ospedale, anche quello pubblico, è infatti chiamato a strutturarsi e a funzionare come qualsiasi altra azienda privata, che deve coprire i propri costi con i ricavi delle prestazioni fornite, assicurando al tempo stesso al malato un servizio con alti standard qualitativi, misurabile sulla base di parametri oggettivi. ¶ Per affrontare con successo i cambiamenti e conseguire i suoi obiettivi istituziona-

li, l'azienda-ospedale deve disporre anche di adeguati strumenti tecnologici, che le consentano di svolgere l'insieme delle sue complesse attività nella maniera più efficiente e razionale. ¶ Supportando la gestione degli aspetti amministrativi e sanitari, come anche le azioni di programmazione, coordinamento e controllo. ¶ Conjugando l'autonomia operativa e funzionale dei singoli servizi, con la massima comunicazione e condivisione informativa. ¶ La soluzione tecnologica proposta dalla Finsiel per le più diverse tipologie di ospedali, sia pubblici che privati, è un sistema informativo completo ed integrato, che rappresenta una soluzione pienamente rispondente alle più attuali esigenze degli ospedali italiani. ¶ Il Sistema Informativo Ospedaliero arricchisce e completa l'offerta Finsiel di soluzioni informatiche per il mondo sanitario, che va dai sistemi di governo ai sistemi per la prevenzione, dalla formazione dei medici ai centri di prenotazione. ¶ Una presenza venticinquennale sul mercato dei sistemi informativi, addici anni di impegno e di applicazione delle tecnologie informatiche in sanità, la conoscenza profonda dei problemi del settore, la professionalità di tremila tecnici ed esperti della società sono il certificato di garanzia dell'offerta Finsiel per gli ospedali e per le altre strutture sanitarie.

Un sistema pensato per chi opera per la salute del cittadino

per il direttore generale costituisce un reale supporto per il governo dell'intero sistema e per un'efficace attività di pianificazione e programmazione

al direttore sanitario permette di organizzare i processi e le attività sanitarie e di controllare la loro qualità

al direttore amministrativo assicura la completa visibilità sulle attività economico-finanziarie dell'ospedale e un sistema di bilancio già orientato al modello aziendale, come ormai impone il nuovo quadro normativo anche per le strutture pubbliche

ai primari e ai responsabili dei servizi permette di controllare le attività del proprio reparto e di valutare la loro qualità, mantenendo e sviluppando l'identità e l'autonomia del reparto nel dialogo con tutte le altre componenti dell'ospedale

ai medici mette a disposizione informazioni assortiti, precise e tempestive per completare il quadro clinico, formulare diagnosi ed elaborare efficaci piani terapeutici

al personale paramedico, che viene sollevato da molti carichi impropri, permette di gestire in modo più efficiente e razionale il proprio lavoro.

1. CD, AD, D: Claudia Neri **PH:** Barry Lewis **DF:** TEIKNA **CL:** Finsiel Italy 1995 Brochure

2. CD, AD, D: Anita Meyer **PH:** Eric Shambroom / Ellen Page Wilson **I, Artist:** Annette Lemieux **Curator:** Judith Hoos Fox **Production Coordinator:** Susan McNally **DF:** Plus Design Inc.
CL: Davis Museum and Cultural Center USA 1994 Brochure

MB

TECHNOLOGY   ASSESSMENT

EXPLOITING TOMORROW'S TECHNOLOGY

ANDERSEN CONSULTING

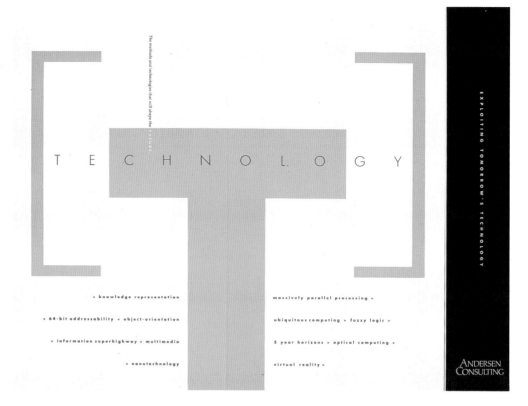

The methods and technologies that will shape the FUTURE.

T E C H N O L O G Y

‹ knowledge representation   massively parallel processing ›

‹ 64-bit addressability ‹ object-orientation   ubiquitous computing › fuzzy logic ›

‹ information superhighway ‹ multimedia   5 year horizons › optical computing ›

‹ nanotechnology   virtual reality ›

EXPLOITING TOMORROW'S TECHNOLOGY

ANDERSEN CONSULTING

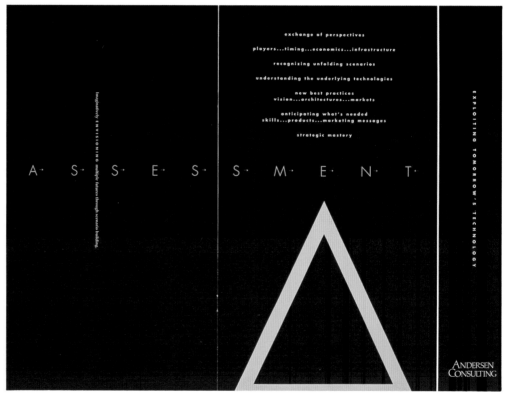

exchange of perspectives

players...timing...economics...infrastructure

recognizing unfolding scenarios

understanding the underlying technologies

new best practices
vision...architectures...markets

anticipating what's needed
skills...products...marketing messages

strategic mastery

Imaginatively ENVISIONING multiple futures through scenario building.

A · S · S · E · S · S · M · E · N · T

EXPLOITING TOMORROW'S TECHNOLOGY

ANDERSEN CONSULTING

CD, AD: Mark Oldach AD, D: Don Emery DF: Mark Oldach Design CL: Andersen Consulting USA 1993 Brochure

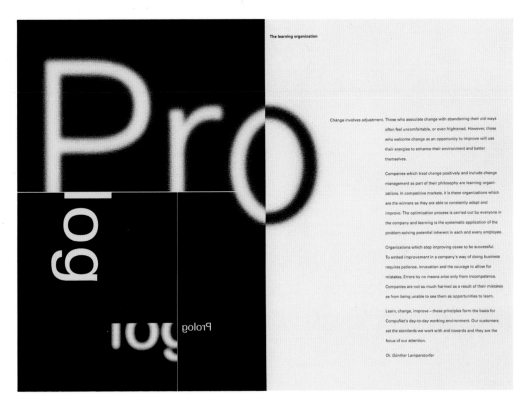

The learning organization

Change involves adjustment. Those who associate change with abandoning their old ways often feel uncomfortable, or even frightened. However, those who welcome change as an opportunity to improve will use their energies to enhance their environment and better themselves.

Companies which treat change positively and include change management as part of their philosophy are learning organizations. In competitive markets, it is these organizations which are the winners as they are able to constantly adapt and improve. The optimization process is carried out by everyone in the company and learning is the systematic application of the problem-solving potential inherent in each and every employee.

Organizations which stop improving cease to be successful. To embed improvement in a company's way of doing business requires patience, innovation and the courage to allow for mistakes. Errors by no means arise only from incompetence. Companies are not so much harmed as a result of their mistakes as from being unable to see them as opportunities to learn.

Learn, change, improve – these principles form the basis for CompuNet's day-to-day working environment. Our customers set the standards we work with and towards and they are the focus of our attention.

Dr. Günther Lamperstorfer

CompuNet®

Annual Report 1994

1. **CD: Christian Boros AD, D: Ing Maak CL: Compunet Computer AG   Germany   1994   Brochure**

2. **CD, AD, D: Klaus Bietz DF: HWL + Partner Design CL: PHAGRO e.V.   Germany   1994   Brochure**

The Book Of Laundromat Etiquette

THE REAL DIRT

(Part of this information was given to us by somebody's mum. So you better believe it).

Separate your clothes into categories (e.g. whites / darks / colours).

Use as few machines as possible. Washers and driers are often under-filled. Incidently one drier will dry three washing machine loads quite comfortably.

Never open someone else's machine, unless you have a death wish.

Go easy on the washing powder. More washing powder does not make the clothes cleaner. This is a myth.

Use the folding bench to fold your clothes, and not the drier, which makes the people waiting get mad.

You can put whites and colours together only if you wash in cold water

Check the pockets for money, tissues, lipstick and pens.

If you wash strange things like your dog or horse blanket please disinfectant the machine you have used, and run the wash through again after you have used it.

Buy bio-degradable washing powder.

If you wander off while your laundry is washing, remember to come back for it. This is not as isolated as it may seem. Unless of course, you don't want it. This is not as isolated as it may seem either.

If you take your clothes out of the dryer and fold them when they're hot, they probably won't need to be ironed.

[Other page] "Nuclear Clean" full screen print. (This page) "Nuclear Clean" embroidery. Code: LL 01 / ML 01

CD, AD, D, PH: Andrew Hoyne PH: Struzina Tomlinson Photography I: Mik Young Kim DF: Andrew Hoyne Design CL: 3 Bags Full   Australia   1994   Booklet

quinze ans. Il était content d'être dans The Fall car il a dû se débarrasser de tous ses automatismes. Il ne pouvait pas comprendre les accords que Craig ou moi jouions bien qu'il sache lire des partitions. C'était vraiment très intéressant.

Tu passes pour une personne très individualiste. Pourquoi alors travailler avec des producteurs ?

Pour moi, pour mes disques, aussi paradoxal que cela puisse paraître, il est essentiel d'avoir l'avis d'une personne extérieure aux chansons. Et puis, je n'ai pas envie de m'embêter à apprendre chaque fois toutes les nouvelles techniques ! Pendant ces dernières années, elles n'ont pas cessé d'évoluer. Dès que je retourne en studio, je me retrouve face à une console différente ou de nouveaux ordinateurs. Lorsque j'ai commencé, il n'y a pourtant pas si longtemps de cela, tout était tellement simple, tout n'était qu'une question de niveau du son, de puissance. Mais, je reste toujours auprès des producteurs, je leur demande de traduire mes idées. C'est amusant, ces gens-là n'ont pas d'ego, aucun d'entre eux ne va clamer haut et fort : *Je suis un ingénieur de génie.* Ce n'est pas leur genre... (Sourire.)

Etais-tu satisfait du travail de John Leckie et Ian Broudie ?

Oh, oui, entièrement. Mais, bon, deux albums, c'est bien suffisant pour eux, non ? (Rires.) Je ne les revois plus. Je peux devenir très agressif en studio. Hum, violent et agressif...

Les rapports que tu pouvais avoir avec Simon Rogers lorsqu'il produisait devaient être différents...

Heu, oui... Mais il vient de m'annoncer qu'il ne travaillera plus jamais avec nous ! (Rires.) Non, non, je sais qu'il le fera si je le lui demande. Il est très fort, mais j'arrivais toujours au studio vers 10 heures du matin, alors qu'un producteur n'attend jamais les musiciens avant 16 heures. Comme ça, je pouvais me permettre de l'espionner. On travaillait ensemble sur des sons, sur la basse et la batterie. J'avais l'impression qu'il jouait à des jeux électroniques mais il me fallait que je prenne soin de lui : je le forçais à prendre des sandwiches et lui demandais de me parler de tous ces gens passionnants avec lesquels il avait eu la chance de bosser, comme Ferry...

Rest en alerte

De toutes les formations que The Fall a pu avoir, as-tu une préférence ?

Hum... Celle qui jouait sur *Shift-work* était vraiment bonne. Tout s'est très bien passé à tous les niveaux, racial aussi ! Les ingénieurs, bien que, d'un point de vue commercial elle n'a pas bien marché... (Soupir.) Cet écœurois là, Kenny Brady, qui jouait du fiddle était vraiment très intéressant. Ceci dit, la formation actuelle est excellente.

J'ai l'impression que tu as trouvé la bonne formule...

Je vois ce que tu veux dire. Plusieurs personnes l'ont fait la même remarque récemment... / Hum, ouais, après tant d'années, j'ai peut-être enfin trouvé ce qu'il me fallait. (Rires.)

Il n'y aura donc plus de changement au sein de The Fall ?

Il y aura toujours des changements, toujours, j'aime ça. Tout simplement parce qu'il ne savaient plus comment jouer de la batterie ! En revanche, je suis certain de ne plus jamais vouloir jouer avec Marc Riley (Silence.) Je sais... Je n'aime pas beaucoup les guitaristes en général. Le seul vrai guitariste, pour moi, c'est Craig (Scanton, dans le groupe depuis 20). De toute façon, les musiciens de The Fall jouent tous de différents instruments, personne n'a le temps de se reposer. C'est une façon de faire entrer de nouvelles idées continuellement, d'être

je dois virer les musiciens, parfois, ils partent d'eux-mêmes. C'est bien d'avoir une formation qui change et évolue. Cela t'empêche de t'endormir, cela te permet de rester continuellement en alerte.

Pourtant, en 1982, au moment de *Hex Enduction Hour*, tu as souhaité un instant mettre fin à l'existence de ce groupe...

Effectivement. *Hex...* devait être le terme de l'aventure. Je l'ai enregistré dans cet état d'esprit, en tout cas. J'en avais marre de toutes ces modes débiles qui se succédaient. D'abord le punk, puis la New Wave, suivie par les New Romantics. Je n'en pouvais plus, j'avais envie de reprendre un boulot normal. On est allé l'enregistrer en partie en Islande. Et puis, l'album, eu un énorme succès...

Ensuite... il paraît que vous avez failli être signé par la Tamla Motown.

C'est vrai ! J'avais les contrats et tout. C'est les gars de Tamla Angleterre qui nous ont contactés. Et puis, ça a coincé avec le grand patron, je crois que c'est Berry Gordy en personne qui a refusé. (Rires.) En fait, *Hex...* est le seul album que j'ai sous la main pour leur envoyer... (Rires.) J'imagine le type de chez Tamla recevant ce mega-contrat avec Tamla Motown et il est parti en fumée ! *Ndlr :* Outre une approche musicale différente des Supremes, Jackson 5 et autres Vandellas, la première chanson de cet album, *The Classical*, contient quelques phrases qui ont dû froisser les gens de Tamla : *"Where are the obligatory niggers? Hey there, fuck-face! Hey there, fuck-..."*

Si tu avais arrêté The Fall, tu aurais pu former un autre groupe après...

Oh, non, certainement pas. Sincèrement, j'aurais cherché un boulot tranquille. Sur l'instant, je ne sais pas exactement ce que j'aurais fait mais les musiciens, nous étions vraiment très jeunes. Les musiciens avaient tous 14 ou 16 ans, je faisais figure d'ancien avec mes 18 ans...

Une nouvelle née

As-tu entendu parler de ce livre, *Something Beginning With O*, qui accorde un long passage aux débuts de The Fall...

Non, ça ne me dit rien. Mais de toute façon, je ne lis pas trop de bouquins sur la musique, toutes ces anthologies. Tant d'années passées dans le milieu, tu deviens un peu aigri face à toutes ces rétrospectives. L'an dernier, aux Etats-Unis, un journaliste voulait faire une grande interview pour un magazine. C'est comme ces énormes livres sur les années 70 ou les années 80, c'est si ennuyeux... Comme ces anthologies sur les poètes. Sincèrement, je ne vois à quoi cela peut servir, j'ai du mal à accepter ce genre d'ouvrages. Je ne peux pas les supporter. Tu vois, c'est exactement la même chose avec ces magazines comme Q ou le Volume... Et puis, je conçois comme si c'était mon premier disque. Selon moi, chaque disque est comme une nouvelle année. Chaque album, je le conçois comme si c'était mon premier disque. Selon moi, c'est la seule façon pour continuer à avancer... C'est peut-être pour cela également que je me débarrasse de tant de musiciens, parce qu'ils veulent toujours revenir à un morceau comme, je ne sais pas moi, *Totally Wired*, par exemple. Cela ne m'intéresse pas du tout. Si tu t'assois et que tu passes ton

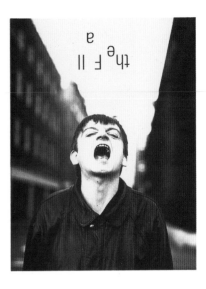

Beastie Boys
Trois mauvais garçons dans le vent.
Photo : Robin

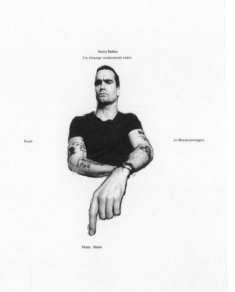

Henry Rollins
Un étrange croisement entre

Kant   et Shwarzenegger.

Photo : Robin

1. CD, AD, D: Pascal Béjean DF: bleu Élastique CL: magic! France 1995 Magazine

2. CD, AD, D: Pascal Béjean DF: bleu Élastique CL: magic! France 1995 Magazine

M

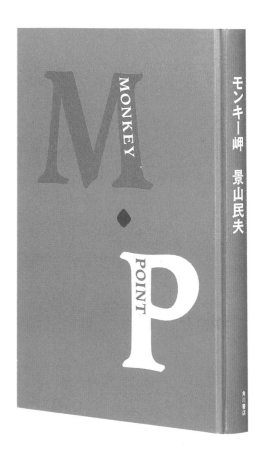

1. AD, I: Keiji Ito D: Shinobu Fukuda CL: Shinchosha Japan 1995 Book cover

2. AD: LopLop Design Inc. D: Mayumi Mitsuki I: Keiji Ito CL: Kadokawa Shoten Japan 1991 Book cover

3. D, I: Hiromasa Mori CL: Shinpusha Japan 1995 Book cover

1. CD, AD, D: Peat Jariya DF: Peat Jariya Design / [Metal] CL: MTU North America   USA   1990   Brochure cover

2. D: Hiroshi Nakajima DF: Plank CL: NTT   Japan   1994   Brochure cover

1. CD, AD, D: Andrew Hoyne   D: Anna Svigos   PH: Dean Phipps   I: Tom Correll   DF: Andrew Hoyne Design   CL: Enzo Presley Ink Design   Australia   1995   Book cover

2. AD, D: Andrew Hoyne   I, DF: Andrew Hoyne Design   CL: Enzo Presley Ink Design   Australia   1994   Book cover

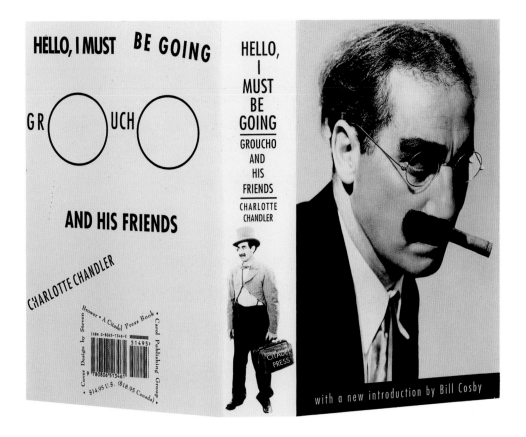

1. AD, D: Steven Brower DF: Steven Brower Design CL: Carol Publishing Group   USA   1992   Book cover

2. CD: Washington Dias Lessa D: Cláudia Siqueira Machado DF: Campos Gerais CL: Editora da Fundação Getúlio Vargas   Brazil   1994   Book cover

1, 2, 3. CD, AD, D: Swifty PH: Will Bankhead DF: Swifty Typografix CL: Gilles Peterson / Red, Hot Organisation / Mo'Wax Records   UK 1994 Flyers

4. CD, AD, D: Swifty DF: Swifty Typografix CL: Straight No Chaser   UK 1994 Flyer

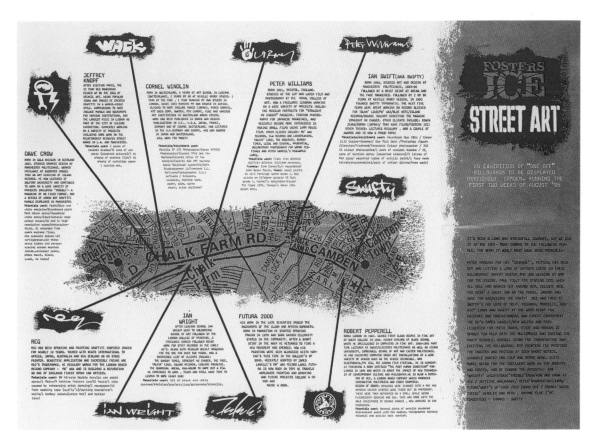

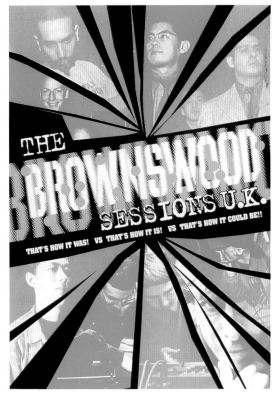

1, 2. CD, AD, D: Swifty PH: Peter Williams DF: Swifty Typografix CL: Fosters Ice / Talkin' Loud UK 1994-95 Leaflet, Flyer

3. CD, AD, D: Swifty DF: Swifty Typografix CL: Swifty Typografix UK 1994 Flyer

OERCION...BLACK IS ONE UNEASY WORD IT ROLLS OFF M
ONGUE AS FAST AND SLICK AS THE COW LICK CLINGING TO YOU
OREHEAD*SHE/I WHISPERED SWEETLILNOTHIN' JESUS BOY BLACK*
ST CAN'T GET ENUFFA YOU REALISE IT COULD BE SOM
NGHEEVER GOT ME GOOD ONLY YOU FORGET, I'D BEEN NEA
HER
HE/I WITNESS/D SOURWILDFLOWER BREAKIN' OF MY HYMEN
NG, BEFORE IT WAS FASHIONABLE I ATE RAW SHELLFIS
UTTING MY FINGERS ON THEIR HIDE SUCKING BONEBLOODJUICE
AITING*SHE/I WALKED THAT DISTANCE SUNLASHED STRETCHI*
ND A HOME. . .

BIBLE HEAVY ON MY ABDOMEN LAMBS TAILS ON THE SPIT BROK
URFEWS TIME AND TIME AGAIN SASHAYING A GIRLIE'S TAWDR
EIGNSHE/I WILLIN' WORKERS HEY SWEETIEPIE WHERE YOU SA
OU FROM. . .CAN'T DO NOTHING 'BOUT' THAT PASTA GIRLIE
ESSON'S LEARNT EVERY SINGLE BLOODIED SUMMER HER IMPRIN
OUND UNDER THE SAME DARK SUBURBAN HEDGE*SHE/I WA*
PEASKING FOR IT THIS HEAVEN SENT FOOD. . .AS UNCERTAIN A
SHADOW THIS GIRL THAT WAS ME TUCKED THE BOONGA
NDER HER BREASTBONE SO IT WOULD HURT AND REMIND HE
ACH TIME*SHE/I WISHED HER SKIN BLACK TOO SUBTLE SMILIN*
ITH SECRETS. . .

AMA'S LITTLE BABY LIKES SHORTNIN, SHORTNIN, MAMA
ITTLE BABY LIKES SHORTNIN BREAD AS SHADOWY UNCERTAINT
HAT GIRL THIS GIRL THAT WAS ME, OOO BABY JUST CAN'T GE
NUFA YOU*SHE/I KNEW THE TASTE OF CUNNINGLIGUISTICS YO*
AWICKED TONGUE. . .EACH TIME THE HURT TUCKED NEATL
NDER HER BREAST AND HICKSVILLE MADE HEARTMEAT AN
ICKSVILLE WAS CLOSE TO THE BONE AND HICKSVILLE'S WHERE I
APPENED*SHE/I TRIED LISTENING TO THE KEENING OF MAMMAL*

OU SEE I WAZ TRYING TO TELL YOU 'BOUT THE TIME IN '8
OUNDABOUT THE TIME 'BLACK AND WHITE WAZ THE NEW
VERYBODY WAZ HOT, WITH JUNGLE FEVER,*SHE/I FELT THE HO*
IND OF HATE BUILDIN' LIKE A SANDSTORM. . .IT WAZ THE TIM
HEN DEEPREDJUICE OF BOYZENBERRIES STAINED OUR TEET
RIMSON SCHOOL WAZ LOOSED FROM OUR RAZZLE TONGUES,*SHE*
LT THE HOT SOUR BREATH OF INFANTILE LUV STRUGGLE WIT

Back

Front

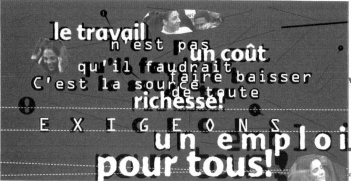

Le groupe communiste de **Livry-gargan**

William Philibert, maire-adjoint
Jean Buisson, maire-adjoint
Jean-Paul Bruscolini, syndic
Samy Cohen, conseiller municipal
Claudie Beaudou, conseillère municipale
et présidente du groupe communiste

vous présentent leurs meilleurs vœux pour l'année 1995

et seraient heureux de vous accueillir
à la réception organisée
le vendredi 27 janvier
à partir de 18 heures
castel Guy Mollet
rond-point des Bosquets
93190 LIVRY-GARGAN

avec le concours de 93 HEBDO / correspondante locale: Nathalie Bonato

1. CD, AD, D: Frédéric Bortolotti DF: Vifargent CL: Groupe Communiste Liury-Gargan France 1995 Leaflet

MB M M

2. AD, D: Andrew Hoyne D: Amanda McPherson PH: Dean Phipps DF: Andrew Hoyne Design CL: John Nicoll Media Australia 1995 Leaflet & Ticket

Front

Back

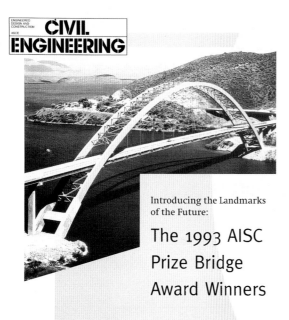

CIVIL ENGINEERING

Introducing the Landmarks of the Future:

The 1993 AISC Prize Bridge Award Winners

A Special Advertising Section In CIVIL ENGINEERING, November 1993

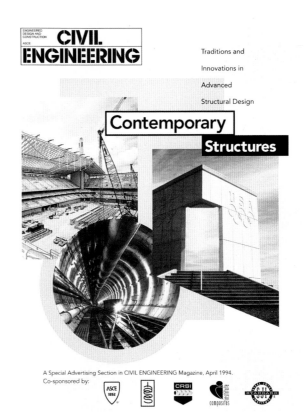

CIVIL ENGINEERING

Traditions and Innovations in Advanced Structural Design

Contemporary Structures

A Special Advertising Section in CIVIL ENGINEERING Magazine, April 1994.
Co-sponsored by:

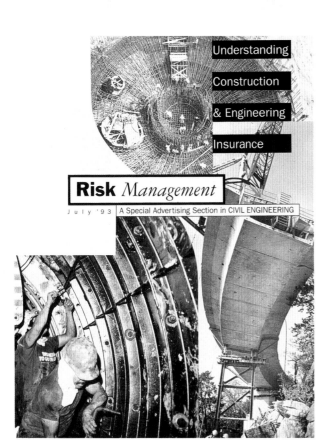

Understanding Construction & Engineering Insurance

Risk *Management*

July '93 A Special Advertising Section in CIVIL ENGINEERING

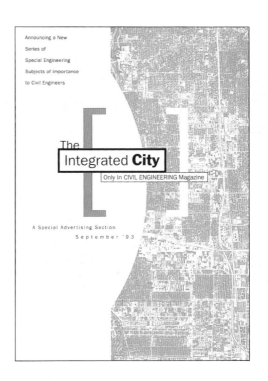

Announcing a New Series of Special Engineering Subjects of Importance to Civil Engineers

The Integrated City

Only In CIVIL ENGINEERING Magazine

A Special Advertising Section
September '93

CD, AD, D: Randy Tibbott DF: Our Designs, Inc. CL: Civil Engineering Magazine USA 1992-93 Leaflet covers

1. AD: Darryl Kenwood CW: Ernest Garcia / Compose, Inc. DF, CL: Darryl Kenwood Design USA 1994 Leaflet

2. CD, AD, D: Kevin Helas DF: Helas Design CL: Artspace/Moving Image Centre New Zealand 1994 Leaflet

CD: OSG CD, AD, D, PH, I: Frédéric Bortolotti DF: The Red Dozer CL: OS Organisation France 1994 Flyers

Who knows what might happen when you get together with lots of people on **Boston Common** for Oxfam America's WORLDFEST and move to hours of **cool tunes**, munch on all kinds of **fabulous food**, lay your eyes and hands on tons of **amazing crafts** and take in a **refreshing global view**? Actually, it's pretty obvious— you'll have a **terrific time!**

Oxfam Worldfest / June 11 and 12 / 11:30am 6:00pm / Boston Common (Park Street end)

for more information call: 617 728 2436

Oxfam America   Tom's OF MAINE

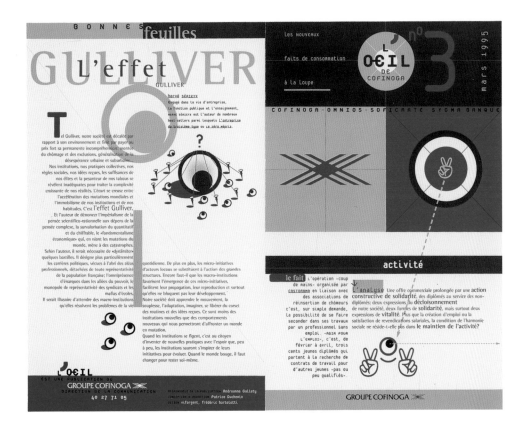

1. CD, AD, D, I: Jane Cuthbertson DF: Myriad Design CL: Oxfam America   USA   1994   Leaflet

2. CD, AD, D, I: Frédéric Bortolotti DF: Vifargent CL: Cofinoga   France   1995   Leaflet

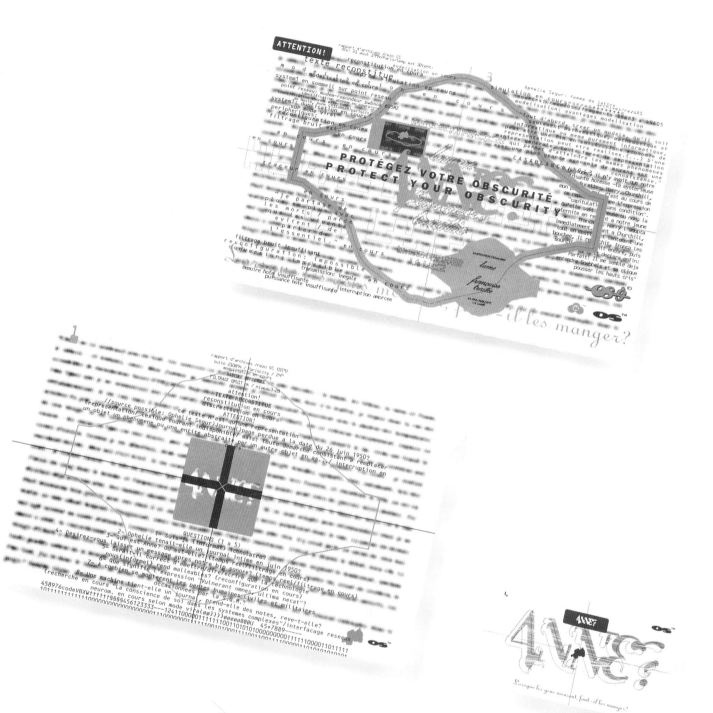

CD, AD, D: Frédéric Bortolotti CD: OSG DF: The Red Dozer CL: OS Organisation France 1995 Flyers

1. CD, AD, D, I: Adele Del Signore PH: Angela Panettieri DF, CL: In-house design for City of Melbourne Environmental Services Australia 1993 Leaflet

2. CD, AD, D, I: Frédéric Bortolotti DF: Vifargent CL: Mattern France 1995 Leaflet

CD, AD, D, I: Pascal Béjean **PH:** Marie-Laure Costa **DF:** bleu Élastique **CL:** AIDES Fédération Nationale   France   1994   **Leaflet**

1. AD: Samuel G. Shelton / Jeffrey Fabian D: Mimi Masse CL: The Langley School   USA   1995   Leaflet

2. CD, AD, D: Paula Benson / Paul West DF: Form CL: Carol Hayes P.R.   UK   1993   Leaflet

1. D, I: Hirosuke Ueno Japan 1995 Flyer

2. D, I: Hirosuke Ueno CL: COLUMBIA Japan 1995 Flyer

3. CD: John Staresinic AD: Dan Cassidy D, I: Ross Gervais DF: Acart CL: Canadian Association of Optometrists Canada 1993 Leaflet

1. AD, D: Samuel G. Shelton / Jeffrey Fabian / Laura Latham DF: KINETIK Communication Graphics, Inc. CL: Whitman-Walker Clinic   USA   1993   Leaflet

2. CD, AD, D, I, CL: Reza Rowhani DF: Reza Rowhani Design   USA   1994   Leaflet

MB

Jesse K. Blackman
Scholarship

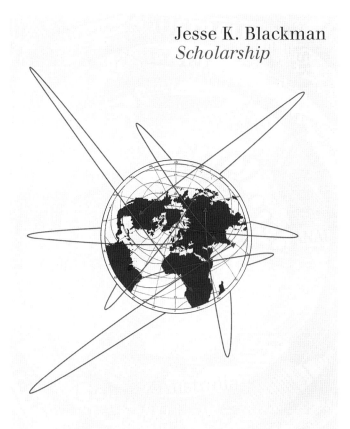

Requirements and Application Form

Vendor
Partnerships

CSC

Leaders in effecting
positive change

1. AD: Jayne Hertko **D, I:** J. Graham Hanson **DF:** American Express Creative Media **CL:** American Express / National Academy Foundation   USA   1994   Leaflet cover

2. CD: Mary Jo Ondrejka **AD, D:** Ramona Hutko **DF, CL:** In-house design by Presentations and Publications Department for Computer Sciences Corporation   USA   1994   Leaflet cover

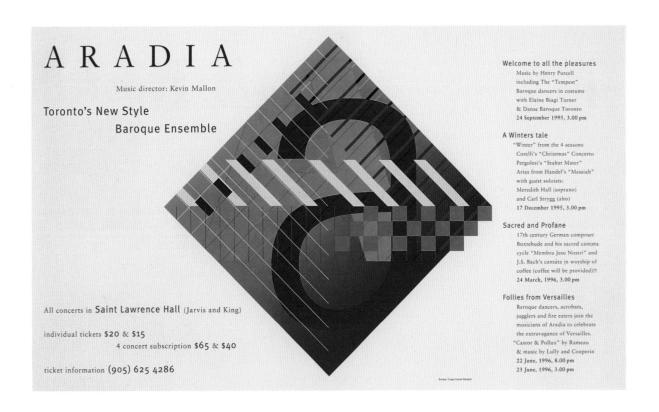

Justus Frantz

Pianist und Dirigent

Kammerphilharmonie *des*
Schleswig-Holstein **Musik**
Festival

Ein Musicon-Konzert.

MUSICON

ABONNEMENT KONZERT

5.

samstag, 5. märz 1994
20 uhr
stadthalle sindelfingen

Scherzo I

Presto con fuoco

Frédéric Chopin, Op. 20

Ivo Pogorelich

Frédéric Chopin
1810-1849
Scherzo h-moll op. 20
Scherzo b-moll op. 31
Scherzo cis-moll op. 39
Scherzo e-Dur op. 54

P A U S E

Modest P. Moussorgskij
1839-1881
Bilder einer Ausstellung
»Promenade«
»Gnomus«
»Das alte Schloss«
»Tuilerien«
»Bydlo«
»Ballett der Küchlein in ihren Eierschalen«
»Samuel Goldenberg und Schmuyle«
»Marktplatz von Limoges«
»Katakomben«
»Die Hütte des Baba Yaga«
»Das große Tor von Kiew«

MUSICON

CD, AD, D: Jochen Rädeker DF: Strichpunkt, Stuttgart CL: Musicon   Germany   1994   Leaflet covers

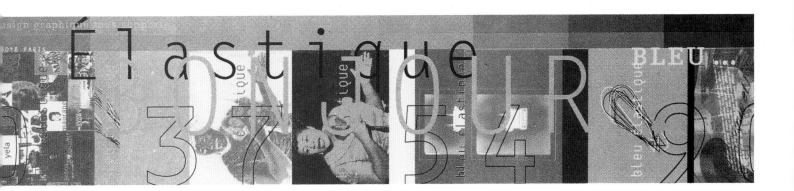

1. CD, AD, D: Pascal Béjean DF, CL: bleu Élastique   France   1994   Flyer

2. D: Kees Wagenaars / Tom Homburg PH: Reinout V/D Bergh / Bas Wilders / Marc Wildner DF: Opera Grafisch Ontwerpers CL: Hig-Centrum Voor Beeldende Kunst en Culture
Netherlands   1995   Leaflet

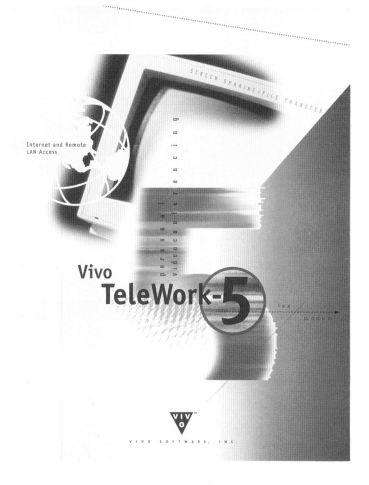

1. CD, AD, D: Claudia Neri DF: TEIKNA CL: Cinecittá International   Italy   1994   Leaflet

2. AD: Kathreen Forsythe D, I: Shannon Beer DF: Forsythe Design CL: Vivo Software, Inc.   USA   1995   Leaflet cover

CD, D: Lluis Jubert CD, AD: Ramon Enrich PH: Ramon Pallarés DF: Espai Grafic CL: Universitat Autonoma de Barcelona Spain 1995 Flyers

MB

CD, AD: James Wai Mo Leung PH: Johnathan Bentham / Carol Rosegg DF: James Leung Design Co. (New York) CL: Michael Mao Dance Company   Hong Kong   1993 Leaflet

D: Eriko Kashiwagi I: Yoko Isono / Takayuki Fujikawa CL: Laforet Harajuku Japan 1992-93 Leaflets

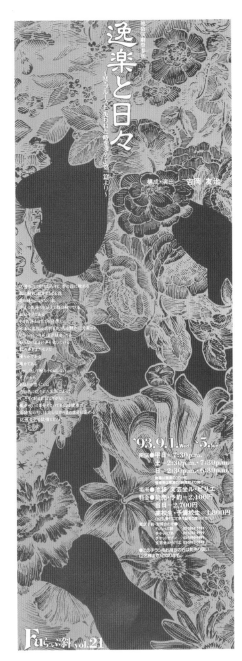

2. CD, AD, D: Jutaro Ito PH: Toshio Kiyofuji DF: Ito Design Inc. CL: Keisho Yoshimura Japan 1991-92 Flyers

1. D: Chiaki Shimizu CL: Fu-Rap Company Japan 1993 Flyer

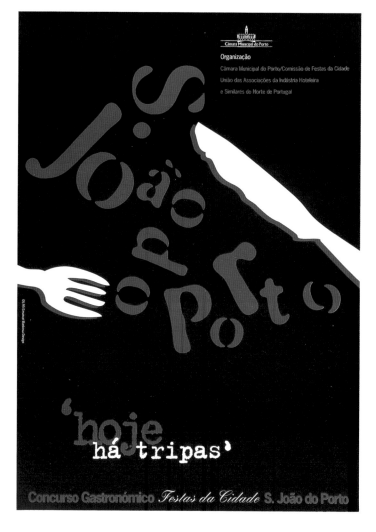

1. D: Kees Wagenaars PH: Erwin Olaf DF: Opera Grafisch Ontwerpers CL: Het Zuidelijk Toneel   Netherlands 1992 Flyer

2. CD, AD, D, I: Emanuel Barbosa DF: Emanuel Barbosa Design CL: Câmara Municipal do Porto   Portugal 1995 Flyer

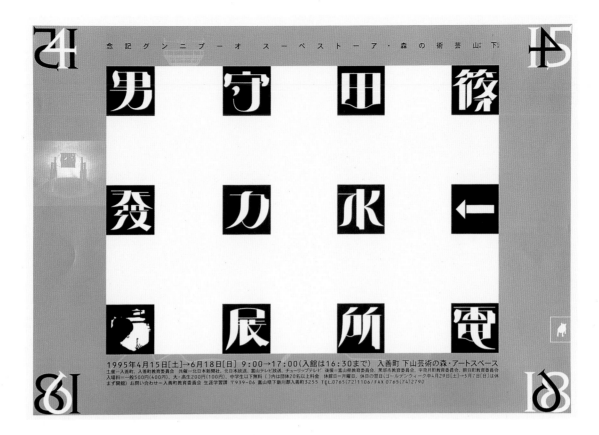

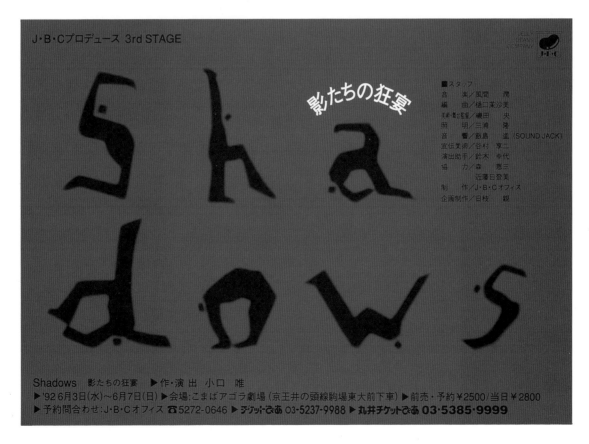

1. CD: Sen Naganawa AD, D: Tadashi Morisaki D: Tadanobu Hara PH: Sadamu Saito / Kazumi Takahashi DF: Flying Rodent Design CL: Nyuzen-machi, Nizayama Forest of Art
Japan 1995 Flyer

2. AD, D, I: Kyoji Tanimura PH: Koichi Terui CL: J・B・C Japan 1992 Flyer

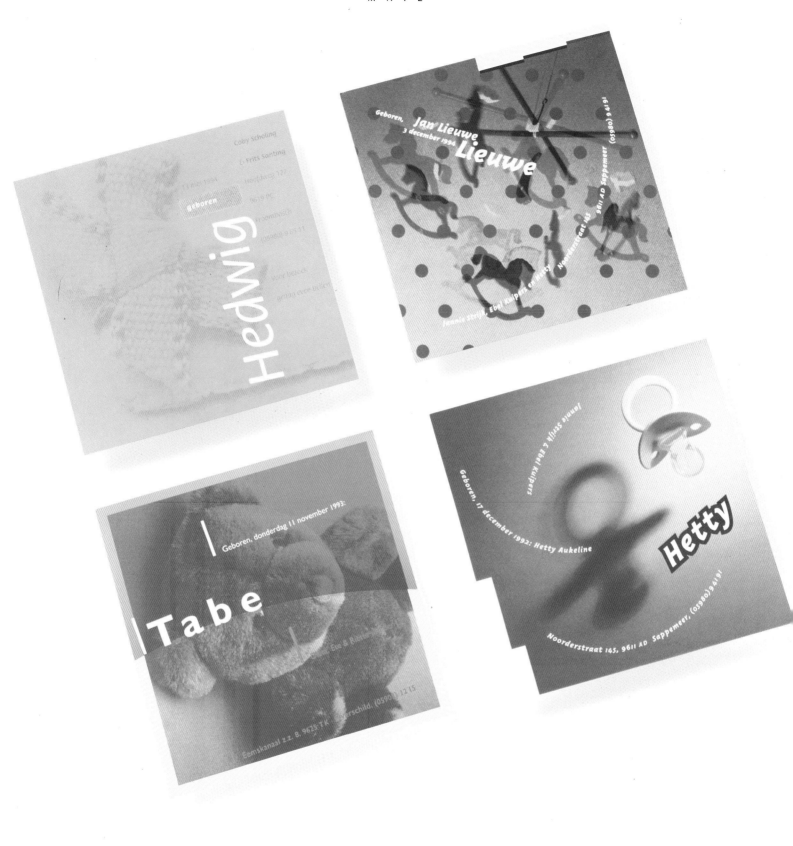

1. D: Ebel Kuipers CL: C. Scholing / F. Santing   2. D, PH: Ebel Kuipers CL: Jannie Strijk / Ebel Kuipers   3. D, PH: Ebel Kuipers CL: Van der Laan Family   Netherlands 1993-94

4. D, PH: Ebel Kuipers CL: Jannie Strijk / Ebel Kuipers Netherlands 1992

1. AD, D, CL: Diane Anderson / Doug Keyes DF: A/D   USA   1994

2. AD, D, PH: Stefanie Choi AD: Susan Dewey DF: NBBJ Graphic Design CL: Columbia Seafirst Center   USA   1993

party...

RAPTURE PROMOTIONS
*(formerly known as RTMP) who
handle Press and Regional radio
for the likes of* **Hut Records***,*
Beechwood Music, Vinyl Japan*,*
Dr Phibes*, the* **Volume** *CDs,*
Drop Nineteens, The Pineapples
and many others....is on the move!

*From Monday August 24th
you can reach us at:
98 St Pancras Way, Camden Town,
London NW1 9NF
Telephone: 071 267 6222
Fax: 071 284 2211*

Colin Simmons

1. CD, AD, D: Paula Benson / Paul West   DF: Form   CL: RTM   UK   1993

2. CD, AD, D: Paul West / Paula Benson   DF: Form   CL: Rapture Promotions   UK   1993

CD, AD, D: Keisuke Unosawa DF: Unosawa Design CL: Jun Co., Ltd. Japan 1992-93

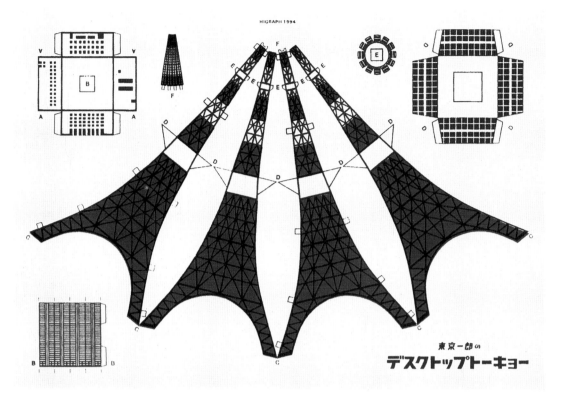

CD: Randy Tibbott AD, D, I: Natasha Lessnik DF, CL: Our Designs, Inc. USA 1992-95

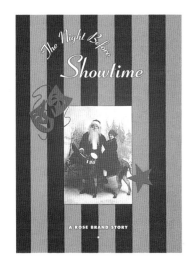

CD, AD, D: Toni Schowalter D: Ilene Price DF: Toni Schowalter Design CL: Rose Brand   USA   1992

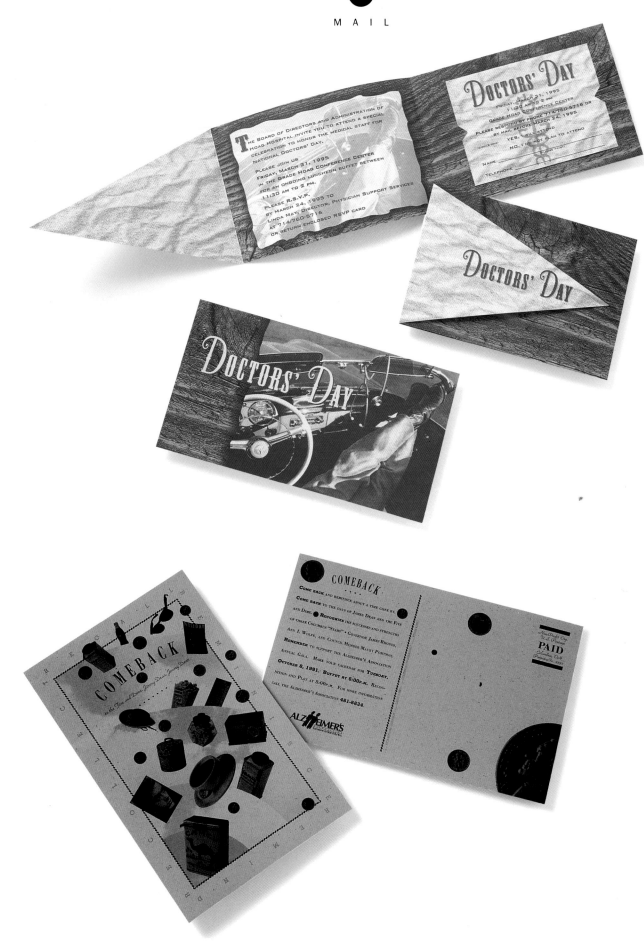

1. CD: Carl Spady D, PH, I: Fred Machuca DF: Hoag Design CL: Hoag Hospital   USA   1994

2. AD, D: Mark Krumel D: Eric Rickabaugh PH: Larry Hamill I: Tony Meuser DF: Rickabaugh Graphics CL: Alzheimer's Association   USA   1991

1994

vous souhaite une bonne année

La Compagnie Bernard Baissait

Compagnie Bernard Baissait 20, rue Rochechouart - 75009 Paris - 40 16 80 12

Experience the **thrill** of world-class tennis with host The John Akridge Companies at the 25th annual Legg Mason Tennis Classic

Wednesday July 20
11:00 am

Suite 14
William H.G. Fitzgerald Tennis Center
16th and Kennedy Streets, NW

RSVP
by July 11, 1994
for you and your guest

Tickets will be at Stadium Box Office Will Call
and are nontransferable

excitement

1. CD, AD, D, DF: Frédéric Bortolotti PH: Daniele F. Fona CL: Compagnie B. Baissait France 1994

2. AD, D: Samüel G. Shelton / Jeffrey Fabian D: Mimi Masse / Scott Rier DF: KINETIK Communications Graphics, Inc. CL: The John Akridge Companies USA 1994

1. CD, AD, D, PH: Jane Cuthbertson DF: Myriad Design CL: Ted Groves / Jane Cuthbertson   USA   1994

2. AD, D: Samuel G. Shelton / Jeffrey Fabian D: Mimi Masse DF: KINETIK Communications Graphics, Inc. CL: Northern Virginia AIDS Ministry   USA   1994

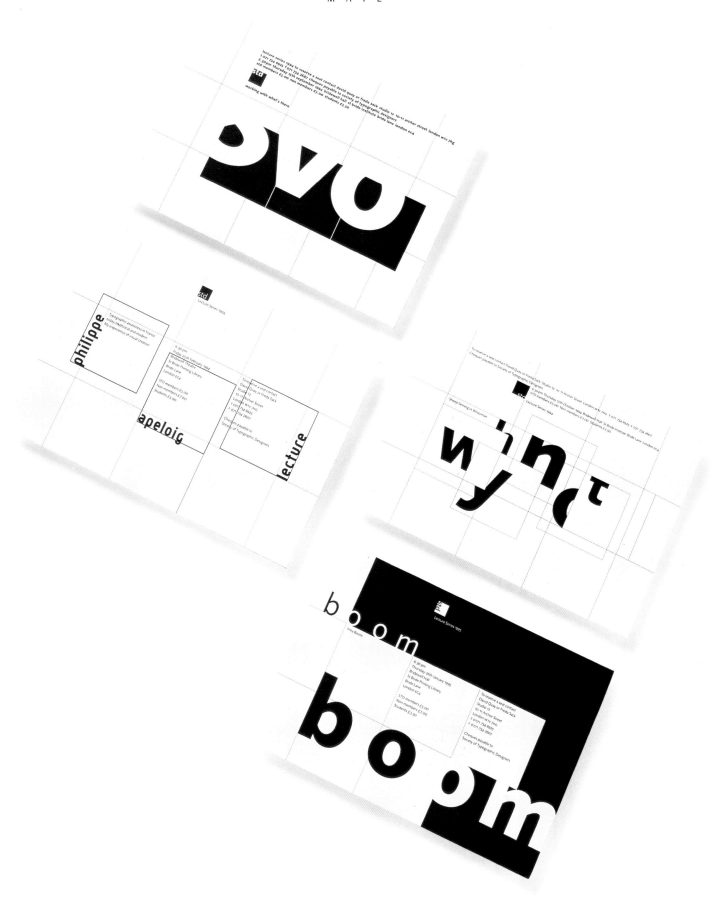

CD, D: David Quay DF: David Quay Design CL: Society of Typographic Designers   UK   1994-95

1. CD, AD, D, I: Frédéric Bortolotti DF: Vifargent CL: Adexchange-Transcan France 1995

2. AD, D: Isabel Augusta / Gustavo Portela DF: Interface Designers CL: Maria Luiza Mendonça Brazil 1993

1. CD: Yoshikazu Tanikawa AD, D: Hidenori Okahashi DF: Lotoath Design Studio CL: Yamato Co., Ltd.   Japan 1995

2. CD: Noriyuki Tanaka AD, D: Hiroaki Konya DF: KOKOKUNOJYO CL: ViBank COSMO Japan 1994

1. CD, AD, D: Yasumasa Yoshioka I: Eri Inoue DF: AZ-Visycom Co., Ltd. CL: Gunze Limited Japan 1995

2. CD, AD, D: Rie Kikkawa CL: Click! Japan 1993

3. CD, AD, D: Rie Kikkawa CL: Lenox Hair Japan 1994

D: Madoka Suemitsu   Japan   1995

CD, AD, D: Toni Schowalter D: Ilene Price DF: Toni Showalter Design CL: CBS Television   USA   1994

COOL

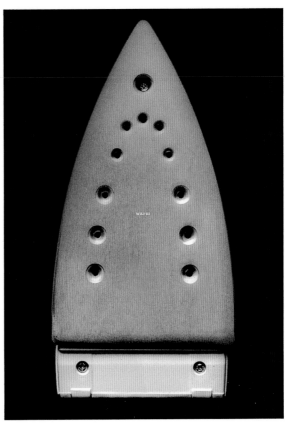

warm

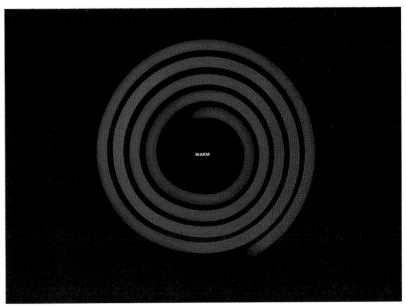

WARM

CD, AD, D: Alan Aboud PH: Sandro Sodano DF: Aboud · Sodano CL: Paul Smith Limited   UK   1992-95

to life.

time

while images
and thoughts
capture only
a moment in

forever

it is the
pure innocence
and genuine
desires of
a newborn
child
that capture
our hearts

1. CD, D: Mark Oldach PH: Anthony Arciero DF: Mark Oldach Design Ltd. CL: Katy Oldach   USA   1994

2. D, I: Mark Fox DF: BlackDog CL: Western Art Directors Club   USA   1994

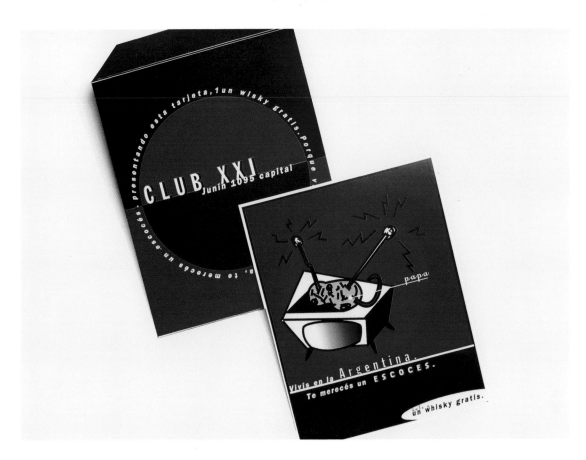

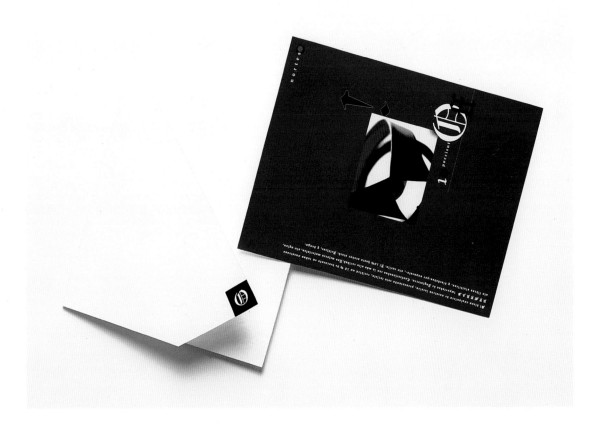

1. CD: Silvio Panizza AD, D: Marcela Augustowsky I: Nino Rodriguez DF: Pandora Box CL: Club XXL PUB   Argentina 1992

2. CD, AD, D: Marcela Augustowsky PH: Virginia Del Giudice DF: Pandora Box CL: Nortes Gentelman's wear   Argentina 1994

CD, AD, D, I: Dave Parmley CD, AD, D: Eric Ruffing DF, CL: 13th Floor   USA   1993   Stationery set

CD, AD, D: Pascal Béjean PH: Gilles Marcodini DF, CL: bleu Élastique   France   1994   Stationery set

CD: Susan Pierson AD, D: Vittorio Costarella DF: Modern Dog CL: Vulcan Northwest   USA   1995   Stationery set

CD, AD, D: Jacques Koeweiden / Paul Postma   PH, CL: Rene Kramers   DF: Koeweiden Postma Associates   Netherlands   1994   Stationery set

CD, AD: Stefan Sagmeister D, I: Eric Zim PH: Tom Schierlitz DF: Sagmeister Inc. CL: Dennis Hayes   USA   1994   Stationery set

CD, AD, D: Stefan Sagmeister PH: Tom Schierlitz DF: Sagmeister Inc. CL: Dennis Hayes   USA   1994   Stationery set

CD, AD: Stefan Sagmeister D, I: Veronica Oh PH: Tom Schierlitz DF: Sagmeister Inc. CL: David Boonshoft   USA   1994   Stationery set

CD: Mark Oldach D: Jennifer Wyville DF: Mark Oldach Design Ltd. CL: American Hospital Association   USA   1995 Stationery set

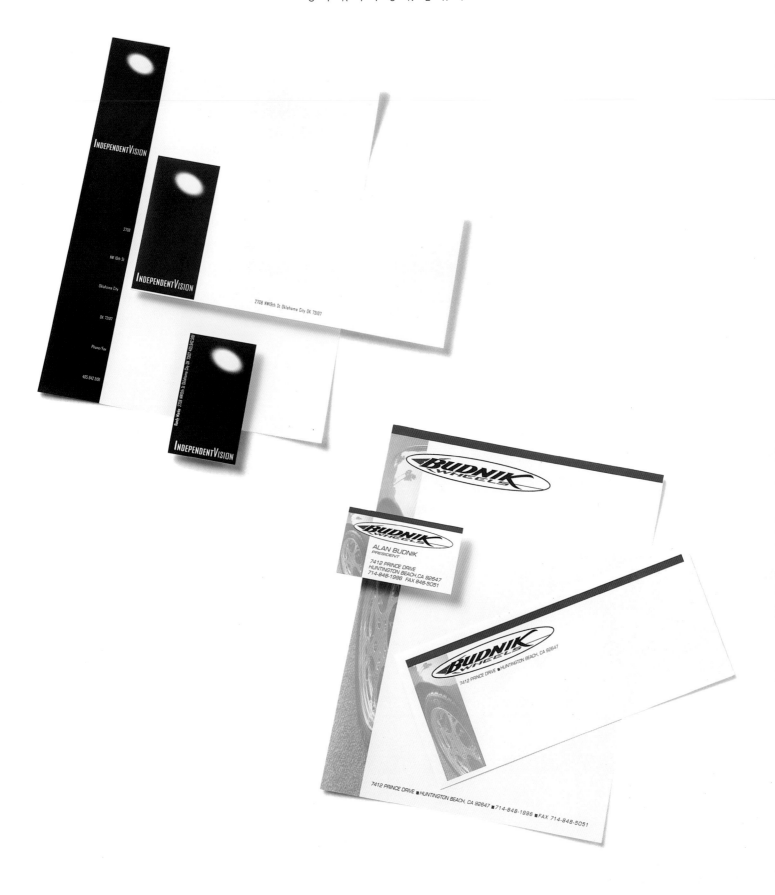

1. CD, AD, D: Peat Jariya DF: Peat Jariya Design / [Metal] CL: Independent Vision   USA   1995   Stationery set

2. CD, AD, D: Alan Middleton PH: Randall Jachmann - Red Zone DF: Middleton Performance Marketing CL: Budnik Wheels   USA   1994   Stationery set

AD, D: Doug Keyes DF: A/D CL: Mike McConnell   USA   1993   Business cards

CD, AD: Jacques Koeweiden / Paul Postma D: Eric Hesen PH: YANi DF: Koeweiden Postma Associates CL: Pim Milo / Richard Meitner / Oswald Schwirtz
Netherlands 1995 Stationery set

1. D: Mimi Masse PH: Annie Adjanavich DF: KINETIK Communications Graphics, Inc. CL: Design Industries Foundation for AIDS, DC USA 1992 Stationery set

2. CD, AD, D: Clifford Cheng DF, CL: Voice Design USA 1994 Stationery set

CD, AD, D: Eric Ruffing PH: Rachel Olsson DF: 13th Floor CL: Sydesis/Syndecrete   USA   1993   Packaging labels

PUT SMOKING OUT OF FASHION

campaign sponsored by The Health Education Authority

CD, AD, D, DF: Stephen Male CL: Health Education Authority   UK   1995   Letterhead

AD, D: Jack Anderson **D:** Lisa Cerveny / Jana Wilson / Julie Keenan **DF:** Hornall Anderson Design Works **CL:** XactData Corporation   USA   1995   Stationery set

CD, AD, D: Jacques Koeweiden / Paul Postma DF: Koeweiden Postma Associates CL: Jaap Stahlie Netherlands 1995 Stationery set

CD, AD, D, PH, I: Frédéric Bortolotti PH: David Gaz DF, CL: The Red Dozer   France   1993-94   Stationery set

CD, AD, D, I: Frédéric Bortolotti   DF, CL: Vifargent   France   1995   Stationery set

S

CD, AD, D: Laurie Kelliher I: Michael Bartalos DF: World Egg CL: Nickelodeon / MTV Networks   USA   1993   Stationery set

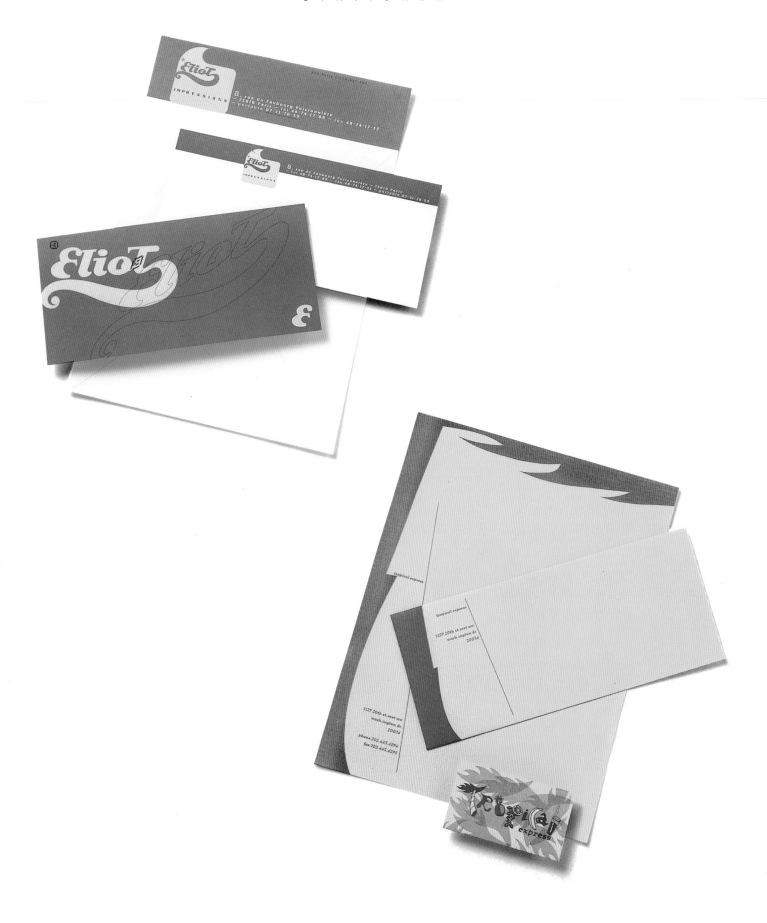

1. CD, AD, D: Frédéric Bortolotti DF: Vifargent CL: Eliot France 1994 Stationery set

2. AD: Samuel G. Shelton / Jeffrey Fabian D: Mimi Masse DF: KINETIK Communication Graphics, Inc. CL: Tropical Express USA 1995 Stationery set

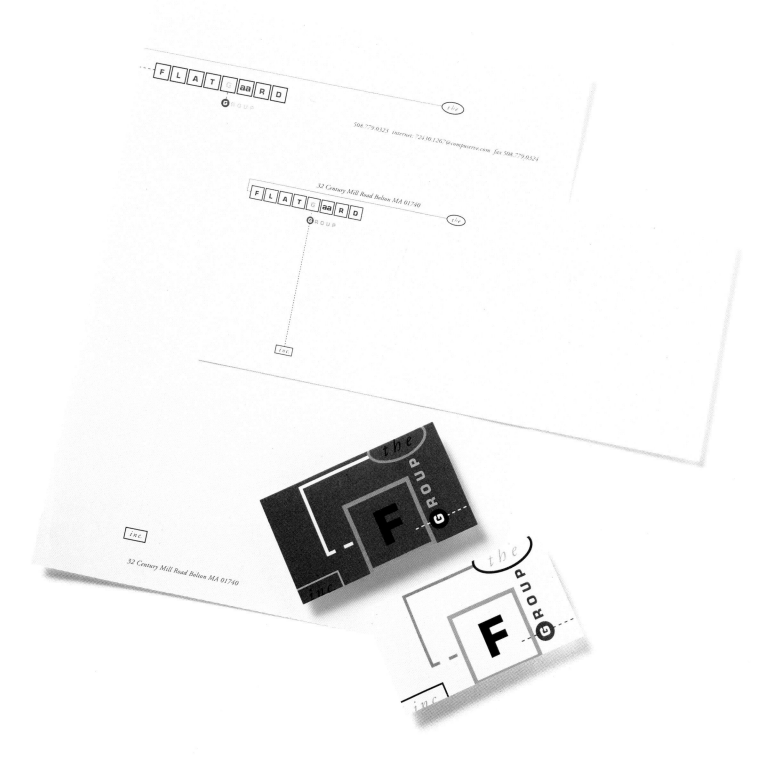

CD: Douglas Eymer D: Laura Hoeting DF: Eymer Design, Inc. CL: Adrian Flatgard   USA   1995   Stationery set

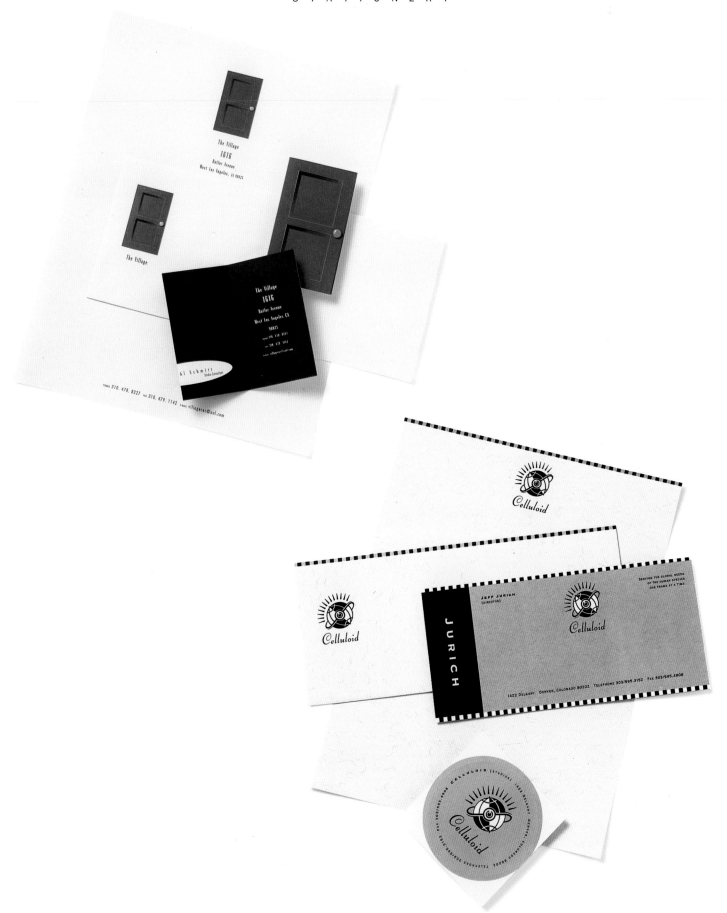

1. CD, AD: Mike Salisbury D: Mary Evelyn McGough I: Rafael Peixoto Ferrira DF: Mike Salisbury Communications Inc. CL: The Village   USA   1995   Stationery set

2. D, I: Mark Fox DF: BlackDog CL: Celluloid Studio   USA   1994   Stationery set

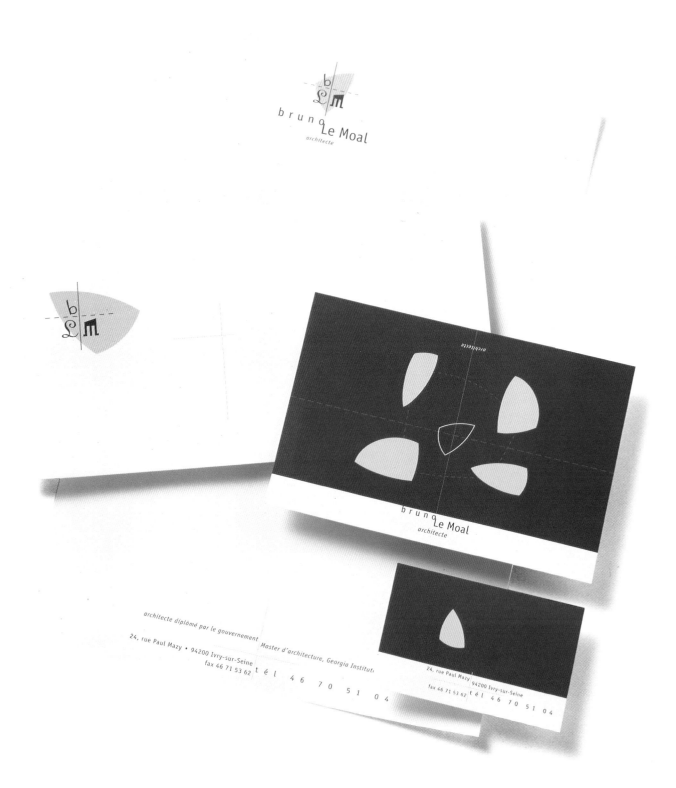

CD, AD, D: Frédéric Bortolotti DF: Vifargent CL: Bruno Le Moal France 1995 Stationery set

1. CD, D, I: Melinda Beck DF: Melinda Beck Studio CL: Nick at Nite   USA   1995   Letterheads

2. CD: Helena Deutsch Almeida Prado AD, D, I: Luiz Henrique S. Cruz DF: L.H.Cruz Design & Fotografia CL: Fofo Comércio e Importação Ltda   Brazil   1995   Stationery set

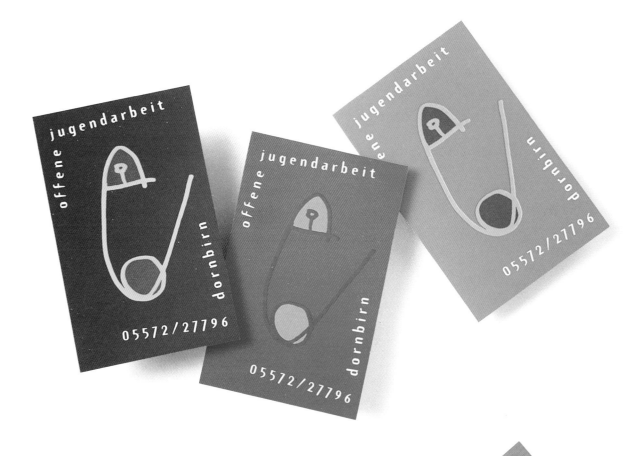

1. CD, D: Kurt Dornig DF: Dornig Grafik Design & Illustration CL: Offene Jugendarbeit Dornbirn   Austria   1995   Name cards

2. AD, D: Yoshihiro Madachi DF: Design Studio Waters CL: Ebony Sounds   Japan   Business card

3. AD, D: Yoshihiro Madachi DF: Design Studio Waters CL: Roof of the Leaf   Japan   1994   Business card

1. CD, AD, D: Robert Bergman-Ungar DF: Bergman-Ungar Associates CL: Wildchild USA 1995 Card

2. D: Ebel Kuipers CL: By De Put Beheer b.v. Netherlands 1994 Business card

3. D, CL: Ebel Kuipers Netherlands 1990 Business card

FROM THE NEW MODERN FARMER ALBUM

HARD ROW TO HOE

RECORDED LIVE ON PIPELINE WITH HOST BOB DUBROW,
WMBR RADIO AT M.I.T., BOSTON: MAY 31, 1994

SHOT DOWN IN FLAMES 4:28
[R.GABRELS / J.RUBIN] © 1994 GABRELS MUSIC ASCAP AND
SAMMY'S GRANDSON'S MUSIC ASCAP

BREAK THE CHAIN 4:15
[J.RUBIN / S.HOLMES / P. MILLIKEN] © 1994 SAMMY'S GRANDSON'S
MUSIC ASCAP / HIGH-LONESOME MUSIC BMI

MODERN FARMER IS: JAMES RUBIN/VOCALS/GUITAR,
REEVES GABRELS/GUITAR/VOCALS,
DAVID HULL/BASS/VOCALS, BILLY BEARD/DRUMS

ENGINEERED BY: CARL PLASTER
MASTERED BY: TONY DAWSEY AT MASTERDISK, N.Y.C.
MANAGEMENT: STEVE CRIST AT CYAN 213.481.2500
ART DIRECTION: 13THFLOOR/ERIC RUFFING

FOR MORE INFORMATION: MONOLYTH ENTERTAINMENT. P.O. BOX 990980
PRUDENTIAL CENTER BOSTON, MA 02199-0980

℗ © 1994 MONOLYTH ENTERTAINMENT, INC. ALL RIGHTS RESERVED. UNAUTHORIZED REPRODUCTION.
PRINTED IN USA.
FOR PROMOTIONAL USE ONLY.
M71307

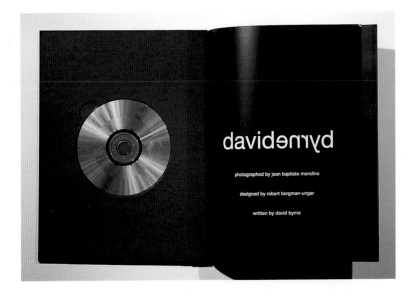

davidbyrne

photographed by jean baptiste mondino

designed by robert bergman-ungar

written by david byrne

CD, AD, D: Robert Bergman-Ungar PH: Jean Baptiste Mondino DF: Bergman-Ungar Associates CL: David Byrne   USA 1995 CD

Delegation

'DARLIN' (I THINK ABOUT YOU)

CD, AD, D, DF: Stephen Male CL: Arista Records UK 1991 Record cover

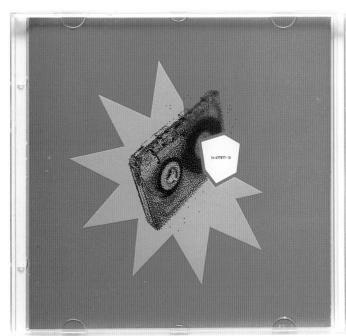

AD, D: Olivier Vandervliet / Nathalie Pollet PH: Maria Dawlat DF: POP X Studio CL: SSR / Crammed Discs Belgium 1994 CD

S F V

Front

Back

AD: Mitsuo Shindo D: Koichi Fujikawa Japan 1992 CD jacket

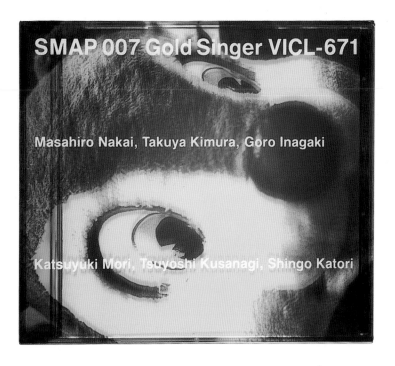

1. AD: Mitsuo Shindo D: Koichi Fujikawa PH: Gen Inaba   Japan   1995   CD jacket

2. AD: Mitsuo Shindo D: Teruyo Ueno   Japan   1994   CD

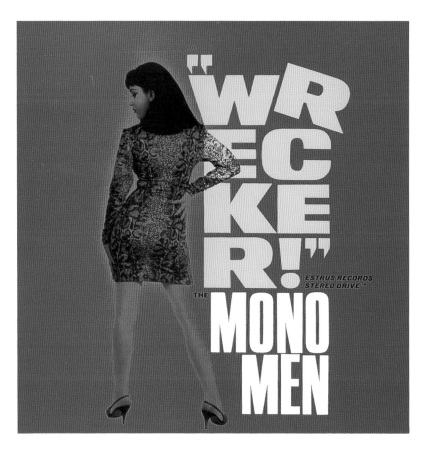

CD: Dave Crider D: Art Chantry PH: Susan McKeever DF: Art Chantry Design CL: Estrus   USA   1993   Record jackets

1. CD: Dave Crider D, DF: Art Chantry CL: Lucky Records   USA   1993   Record jacket

2. D: Art Chantry DF: Art Chantry Design CL: Moe's Mo'Rockin' Cafe   USA   1995   Record (and poster)

Front

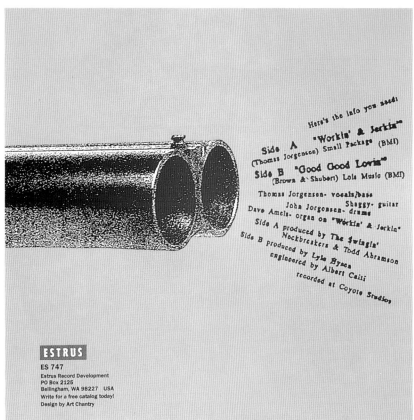

Back

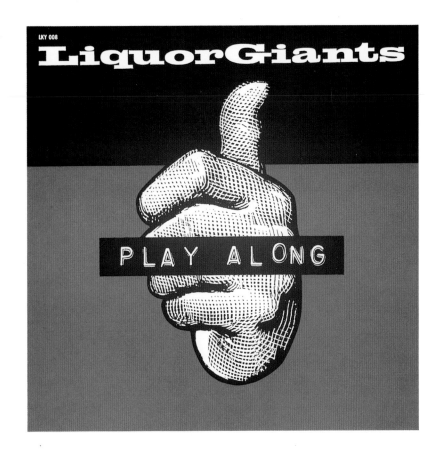

1. D, DF: Art Chantry CL: Lucky Records USA 1994 Record cover

2. AD, D: Tycoon Graphics I: Naoyuki Suzuki CL: Groovin' High Japan 1993 Record jacket

Front

Back

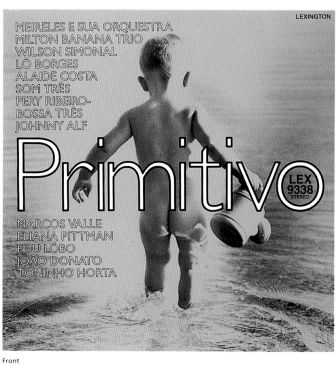

Front

Back

AD, D: Yoshihiro Madachi PH: Voller Ernst / Megapress I: Kate Marinefield DF: Design Studio Waters CL: Lexington Co., Ltd.   Japan 1994 Record jackets

Front

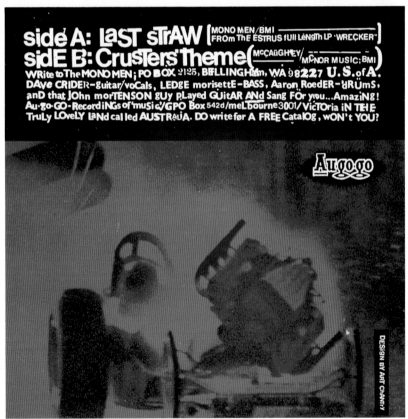

Back

CD: Dave Crider D, DF: Art Chantry CL: Augogo   USA   1993   Record jacket

1. CD: Masaaki Kato AD, D: Eiichi Sakota D: Toshio Kawakami / Yoshitaka Shinmori DF: Rec 2nd. CL: FM Osaka Co., Ltd. Japan 1994 Carrier bag

2. CD, AD: Sayuri Takahata D: Kaoru Matsui / Noriko Kubo I: Sarry. T CL: MYCAL HONMOKU Japan 1995 Carrier bag

1. AD, D: Masayoshi Nakajo D: Midori Yonezawa CL: The Ginza Co., Ltd.   Japan   1995   Carrier bag

2. AD, D: Sergio Liuzzi / Gustavo Portela DF: Interface Designers CL: Celeiro   Brazil   1991   Packaging

2. D, I: Mark Fox D: Paul Huber DF: BlackDog CL: C-Cube Microsystems   USA   1990   Packaging

1. AD, D: Andrew Hoyne PH: Rob Blackburn DF: Andrew Hoyne Design CL: Just Jeans   Australia   1994   Shoe packaging

1. CD, D, PH: Marcia Romanuck D: Fran Mckay DF: The Design Company CL: Metropolis Fine Confections   USA 1995 Packaging

2. AD, D: Sérgio Liuzzi AD, D, I: Gustavo Portela DF: Interface Designers CL: Parmê-Restaurant Brazil 1994 Packaging

1. CD, AD, D, I: John Sayles DF: Sayles Graphic Design CL: Des Moines Art Center   USA   1994   Carrier bag

2. CD, AD, D, I: Marcia Romnuck PH: Barry Aronson DF: The Design Company CL: Route 66 Southwestern Foods   USA   1990   Packaging

1. CD: Rachel Rutherford AD, D, I: John Sayles DF: Sayles Graphic Design CL: ImMIX   USA   1992   Packaging

2. AD, D: Sérgio Liuzzi / Gustavo Portela DF: Interface Designers CL: Celeiro   Brazil   1991   Packaging

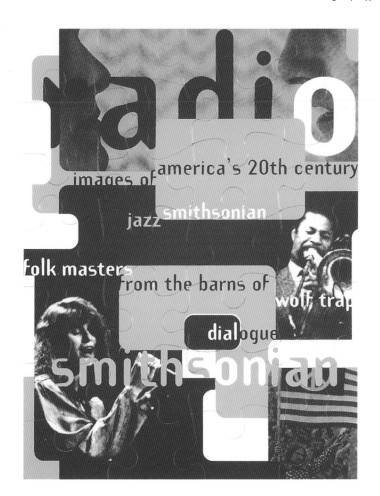

1. AD, D: Samuel G. Shelton / Jeffrey Fabian D: Mimi Masse DF: KINETIK Communication Graphics, Inc. CL: Smithsonian Institution   USA   1994   Puzzle

2. CD, AD, D: Jacques Koeweiden / Paul Postma CD, PH: YANi DF: Koeweiden Postma Associates CL: Ministry of Economic Affairs   Netherlands   1993   Calendar

The 1995 **RCAP/MESA** *Calendar*

Children are our most valuable natural resource. —Herbert Hoover

may

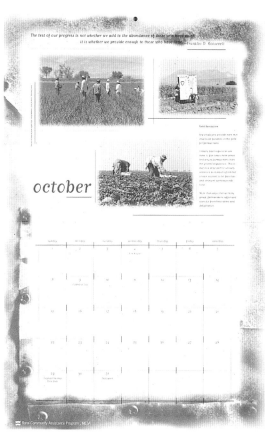

The test of our progress is not whether we add to the abundance of those who have much; it is whether we provide enough to those who have little. —Franklin D. Roosevelt

october

AD, D: Samuel G. Shelton / Jeffrey Fabian D: Mimi Masse PH: Davida Johns / Celia Roberts DF: KINETIK Communication Graphics, Inc. CL: Rural Community Assistance Program

USA 1994 Calendar

バレンタインデー

February						
s.	m.	t.	w.	t.	f.	s.
			1	2	3	4
5	6	7	8	9	10	11
12	13	14	15	16	17	18
19	20	21	22	23	24	25
26	27	28				

Father's Day

June						
s.	m.	t.	w.	t.	f.	s.
			1	2	3	4
5	6	7	8	9	10	11
12	13	14	15	16	17	18
19	20	21	22	23	24	25
26	27	28	29	30		

バカンス計画

July						
s.	m.	t.	w.	t.	f.	s.
					1	2
3	4	5	6	7	8	9
10	11	12	13	14	15	16
17	18	19	20	21	22	23
24	25	26	27	28	29	30
31						

2. CD: Ikko Tanaka / Kazuko Koike AD, D: Masaaki Hiromura D: Nobuhiko Aizawa I: Iku Akiyama DF: Hiromura Design Office, Inc. CL: Ryohinkeikaku Co., Ltd.
Japan 1994 Calendars

1. CD, AD: Sayuri Takahata D: Kaoru Matsui / Noriko Kubo CL: MYCAL HONMOKU Japan 1995 POP displays

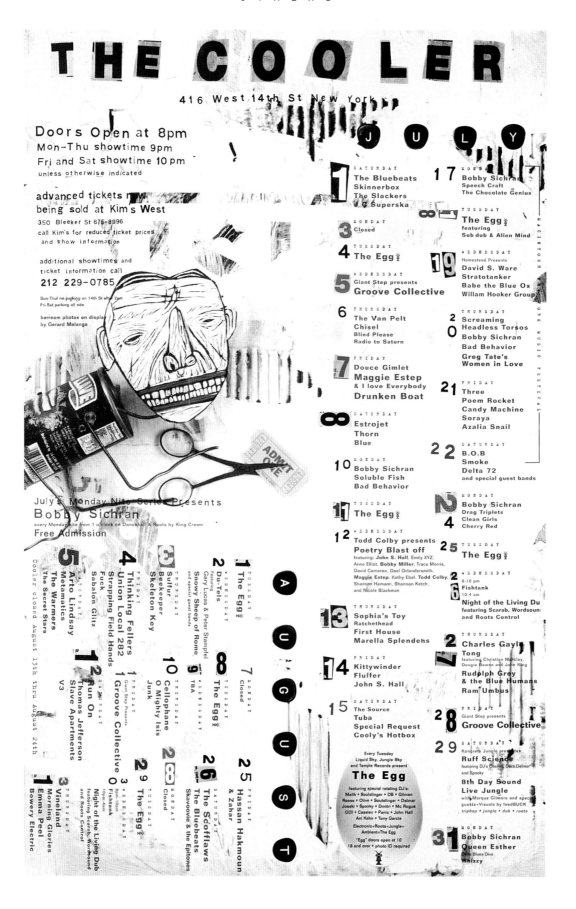

Index of
Submittors

1, 2 & 3 COLOR GRAPHICS Vol.2

1・2・3色 グラフィックス 2

Jacket Design

Douglas Gordon

Art Director

Yutaka Ichimura

Editor

Yuko Yoshio

Business Manager

Masato Ieshiro

Photographer

Kuniharu Fujimoto

Coordinators

Chizuko Gilmore (San Francisco)

Clive Avins, Kimiko Avins (London)

English Translator & Consultant

Sue Herbert

Publisher

Shingo Miyoshi

1996年1月31日初版第1刷発行

定価 16,000円（本体15,534円）

発行所 ピエ・ブックス

〒170 東京都豊島区駒込4-14-6-301

TEL: 03-3949-5010 FAX: 03-3949-5650

印刷／製本 エバーベスト・プリンティング（株）

Printed and Bound by Everbest Printing Co., Ltd.

Ko Fai Industrial Building, Block C5, 10th Floor,

7 Ko Fai Road, Yau Tong, Kowloon, Hong Kong

Tel: 852-2727-4433 Fax: 852-2772-7908

ISBN 4-938586-93-2 C3070 P16000E

BROCHURE & PAMPHLET COLLECTION 1
Pages: 224(144 in color) ¥15,000
業種別カタログ・コレクション
Here are hundreds of the best brochures
and pamphlets from Japan.
This collection will make a valuable
sourcebook for anyone involved in
corporate identity advertising and
graphic design.

LABELS AND TAGS
Pages: 224(192 in color) ¥15,000
ファッションのラベル&タグ・コレクション
Over 1,600 garment labels representing
450 brands produced in Japan are
included in this full-color collection.

COVER TO COVER
Pages: 240(176 in color) ¥17,000
世界のブック&エディトリアル・デザイン
The latest trends in book and magazine
design are illustrated with over 1,000
creative works by international firms.

BUSINESS STATIONERY GRAPHICS 1
Pages: 224(192 in color) ¥15,000
世界のレターヘッド・コレクション
Creatively designed letterheads,
business cards, memo pads, and other
business forms and documents are
included this international collection.

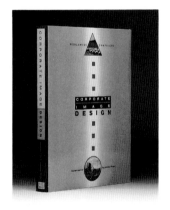

CORPORATE IMAGE DESIGN
Pages: 336(272 in color) ¥16,000
世界の業種別CI・ロゴマーク
This collection presents the best
corporate identity projects from around
the world. Creative and effective designs
from top international firms are featured
in this valuable source book.

POSTCARD GRAPHICS 3
Pages: 232(208 in color) ¥16,000
世界の業種別ポストカード・コレクション
Volume 3 in the series presents more
than 1,200 promotional postcards in
dazzling full color. Top designers from
the world over have contributed to this
useful image bank of ideas.

GRAPHIC BEAT London / Tokyo 1 & 2
Pages: 224(208 in color) ¥16,000
音楽とグラフィックのコラボレーション
1,500 music-related graphic works from
29 of the hottest designers in Tokyo and
London. Features Malcolm
Garrett,Russell Miles, Tadanori Yokoo,
Neville Brody, Vaughn Oliver and others.

BUSINESS CARD GRAPHICS 2
Pages: 224(192 in color) ¥16,000
世界の名刺&ショップカード、第2弾
This latest collection presents 1,000
creative cards from international
designers. Features hundreds of cards
used in creative fields such as graphic
design and architecture.

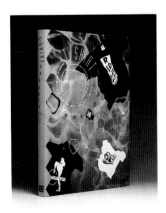

T-SHIRT GRAPHICS
Pages: 224(192 in color) ¥16,000
世界のTシャツ・グラフィックス
This unique collection showcases 700
wonderfully creative T-Shirt designs from
the world's premier design centers.
Grouped according to theme, categories
include sports, casual, designer and
promotional shirts among others.

DIAGRAM GRAPHICS
Pages: 224(192 in color) ¥16,000
世界のダイアグラム・デザインの集大成
Hundreds of unique and lucid
diagrams,charts, graphs, maps and
technical illustrations from leading
international design firms. Variety of
media represented including computer
graphics.

SPECIAL EVENT GRAPHICS
Pages: 224(192 in color) ¥16,000
世界のイベント・グラフィックス特集
This innovative collection features design
elements from concerts, festivals, fashion
shows, symposiums and more.
International works include posters,
tickets, flyers, invitations and various
premiers.

RETAIL IDENTITY GRAPHICS
Pages: 208(176 in color) ¥14,800
世界のショップ・グラフィックス
This visually exciting collection
showcases the identity design campaigns
of restaurants, bars, shops and various
other retailers. Wide variety of pieces are
featured including business cards, signs,
menus, bags and hundreds more.

PACKAGING DESIGN & GRAPHICS 1
Pages: 224(192 in color) ￥16,000
世界の業種別パッケージ・デザイン
An international collection featuring 400 creative and exciting package designs from renowned designers.

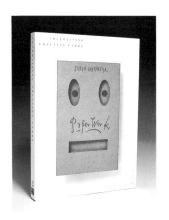

ADVERTISING GREETING CARDS 3
Pages: 224(176 in color) ￥16,000
世界のダイレクトメール集大成、第3弾
The best-selling series continues with this collection of elegantly designed advertising pieces from a wide variety of categories. This exciting image bank of ideas will interest all graphic designers and direct mail specialists.

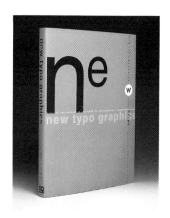

NEW TYPO GRAPHICS
Pages: 224(192 in color) ￥16,000
世界の最新タイポグラフィ・コレクション
New and innovative typographical works gathered from top designers around the world. A wide variety of type applications are shown including posters, brochures, CD jackets, calendars, book designs and more.

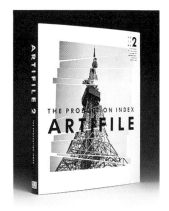

The Production Index ARTIFILE 2
Pages: 244(240 in color) ￥13,500
活躍中！最新プロダクション年鑑、第2弾
A design showcase featuring the best works from 115 graphic design studios, photographers, and creators in Japan. Works shown include print advertisements, corporate identity pieces, commercial photography and illustration.

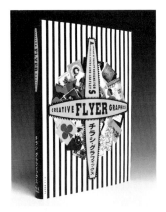

CREATIVE FLYER GRAPHICS
Pages: 224(176 in color) ￥16,000
チラシ・グラフィックス
Features about 500 rigorously screened flyers and leaflets. You see what superior graphics can accomplish on a single sheet of paper. This is an invaluable reference to all your advertising production for years to come.

1, 2 & 3 COLOR GRAPHICS
Pages: 208(Full Color) ￥16,000
1・2・3色 グラフィックス
See about 300 samples of 1,2 & 3 color artwork that are so expressive they often surpass the impact of full 4 color reproductions. This is a very important book that will expand the possibilities of your design works in the future.

LABELS AND TAGS 2
Pages: 224(192 in color) ￥16,000
世界のラベル＆タグ・コレクション　2
This long-awaited second volume features 1500 samples representing 400 top name-brands from around the world.

BROCHURE DESIGN FORUM 2
Pages: 224(176 in color) ￥16,000
世界の最新カタログ・コレクション　2
Features 70 businesses and 250 reproductions for a complete overview of the latest and best in brochure design.

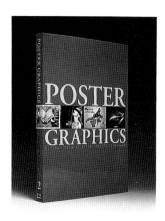

POSTER GRAPHICS 2
Pages: 256(192 in color) ￥17,000
業種別世界のポスター集大成
700 posters from the top creators in Japan and abroad are showcased in this book - classified by business. This invaluable reference makes it easy to compare design trends among various industries and corporations.

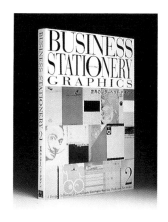

BUSINESS STATIONERY GRAPHICS 2
Pages: 224(192 in color) ￥16,000
世界の業種別レターヘッド・コレクション、第2弾
The second volume in our popular "Business Stationery Graphics" series. This publication focuses on letterheads, envelopes and business cards, all classified by business. This collection will serve artists and business people well.

SENSUAL IMAGES
Pages: 208(98 in color) ￥4,800
世界の官能フォト傑作集
We selected the best sensual works of 100 photographers from all over the world. The result is 200 sensual images concentrated in this volume. Page after page of photos that will quicken your pulse and stimulate your fantasies!

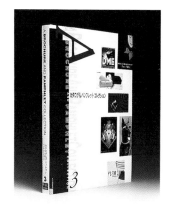

BROCHURE & PAMPHLET COLLECTION 3
Pages: 224(176 in color) ￥16,000
好評！業種別カタログ・コレクション、第3弾
The third volume in "Brochure & Pamphlet" series. Sixteen types of businesses are represented through artwork that really sell. This book conveys a sense of what's happening now in the catalogue design scene. A must for all creators.

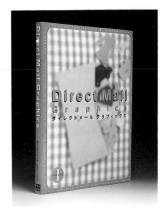

DIRECT MAIL GRAPHICS 1
Pages: 224(176 in color) ￥16,000
衣・食・住のセールスＤＭ特集！
The long-awaited design collection featuring direct mailers with outstanding sales impact and quality design. 350 of the best pieces, classified into 100 business categories. A veritable textbook of current direct marketing design.

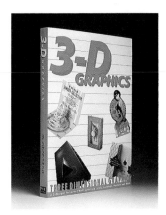

3-D GRAPHICS
Pages: 224(192 in color) ￥16,000
３−Ｄ・グラフィックスの大百科
300 works that demonstrate the best possibilities of 3-D graphic methods, including DMs, catalogues, posters, POPs and more. The volume is a virtual encyclopedia of 3-D graphics.

The Production Index ARTIFILE 3
Pages: 224(Full color) ￥13,500
活躍中！最新プロダクション年鑑、第３弾
Contributors are 116 top production companies and artists. See the artwork and read insightful messages from the creators.

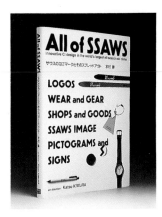

ALL OF SSAWS
Pages: 120(Full color) ￥8,800
ザウスのＣＩ、アプリケーション＆グッズ
The graphics of SSAWS - the world's No.1 all-season ski dome is showcased in this publication; everything from CI and rental wear to notions and signs. This is the CI concept of the future - design that changes, evolves and propagates freely.

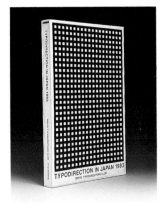

TYPO-DIRECTION IN JAPAN 5
Pages: 254(183 in color) ￥17,000
年鑑 日本のタイポディレクション'９３
314 award-winning typographic works from around the world are shown in this book. It includes recent masterpieces by eminent art directors and designers as well as powerful works by up-and-comoing designers.

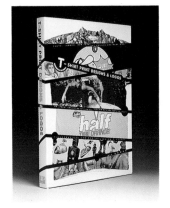

T-SHIRT PRINT DESIGN & LOGOS
Pages: 224(192 in color) ￥16,000
世界のＴシャツ・プリントデザイン＆ロゴ
Volume 2 of our popular "T-shirt Graphics" series. In this publication, 800 designs for T-shirt graphics, including many trademarks and logotypes are showcased. The world's top fashion makers are featured.

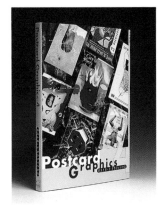

POSTCARD GRAPHICS 4
Pages: 224(192 in color) ￥16,000
世界の業種別ポストカード・コレクション
Our popular Postcard Graphics series has been revamped for Postcard Graphics Vol.4. This new-look volume showcases approximately 1,000 varied examples selected from the world's best and ranging from direct mail to private greeting cards.

SPORTS GRAPHICS
Pages: 224(192 in color) ￥16,000
世界のスポーツ用品グラフィックス
An up-beat collection of 1,000 sporting-goods graphics from all around the world. This book features a variety of different goods, including uniforms, bags, shoes and equipment, and covers all sorts of sports: soccer, basketball, skiing, surfing and many, many more.

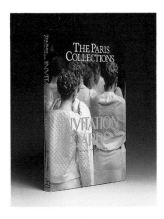

The Paris Collections / INVITATION CARDS
Pages: 200(192 in color) ￥16,000
パリ・コレクションの招待状グラフィックス
The Paris Collections are renowned for style and sophistication. Individual designers present their collections, and this volume features about 430 invitation cards for these shows, each mirroring the prestige and originality of the fashion house, and together encapsulating the glamour of Paris.

COMPANY BROCHURE COLLECTION
Pages: 224(192 in color) ￥16,000
業種別（会社・学校・施設）案内グラフィックス
Private companies, schools and leisure facilities - 220 informative brochures and guides, classified by type of business, from all sorts of enterprises and facilities throughout Japan. A fascinating and useful catalogue of imaginative layouts combined with effective design.

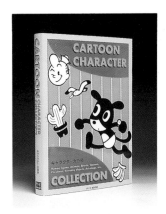

CARTOON CHARACTER COLLECTION
Pages: 480(B/W) ￥9,800
キャラクター大百科
A selection of 5,500 carefully chosen, quality cartoon drawings from the most successful illustrators in the business. Conveniently classified, the drawings cover everything from animals and natural scenery to food, sports and seasonal images. An encyclopedic collection and a useful source book.

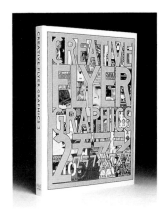

CREATIVE FLYER GRAPHICS 2
Pages: 224(208 in color) ￥16,000
世界のチラシ・グラフィックス２
This follow-up volume presents around 600 different flyers and leaflets promoting just about everything! From information on arts and music to advertising of food, consumer products and package tours, this selection demonstrates the power-packed design features of promotional flyers.

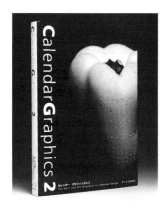

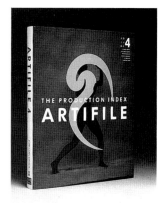

CALENDAR GRAPHICS 2
Pages: 224(192 in color) ¥ 16,000
カレンダー・デザイン集の決定版、第2弾
A second volume of calendar graphics
bring together 250 examples of artwork
for '94 and '95 retail and corporate
publicity calendars collected worldwide.

DIAGRAM GRAPHICS 2
Pages: 224(208 in color) ¥ 16,000
世界のダイアグラム・デザイン特集、第2弾
From computer-assisted 'new wave'
graphics to the more orthodox, hand-
drawn diagrams, a compendium of the
latest and best graphics, maps, charts
and illustrations from all over the world.
A 'must' for every designer's bookshelf !

CORPORATE PROFILE GRAPHICS
Pages: 224(204 in color) ¥ 16,000
世界の会社案内グラフィックス
An unparalleled, international collection of
corporate brochures, catalogues and guides
for schools and leisure facilities, and
organization profiles, selected for
excellence in design and presentation, and
conveniently classified by type of business.

The Production Index ARTIFILE 4
Pages: 224(218 in color) ¥ 12,500
活躍中！最新プロダクション年鑑、第4弾
A portfolio of recent representative work
from 107 of the most influential Japanese
production companies and designers. An
invaluable source book to keep up with
the latest developments in the graphics
scene in Japan.

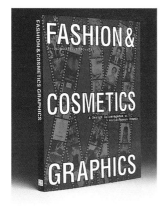

FASHION & COSMETICS GRAPHICS
Pages: 224(208 in color) ¥ 16,000
世界のファッション&化粧品・グラフィックス特集
A unique selection of promotional material
for 40 top brand names in clothes,
accessories, and cosmetics. 800 entries
encompassing graphic design at the
forefront of fashion.

カタログ・新刊のご案内について
総合カタログ、新刊案内をご希望の方は、はさみ込みのアンケートはがきを
ご返送いただくか、90円切手同封の上、ピエ・ブックス宛お申し込み下さい。

CATALOGUES ET INFORMATIONS SUR LES NOUVELLES
PUBLICATIONS
Si vous désirez recevoir un exemplaire gratuit de notre catalogue général
ou des détails sur nos nouvelles publications, veuillez compléter la carte
réponse incluse et nous la retourner par courrierou par fax.

CATALOGUES AND INFORMATION ON NEW PUBLICATIONS
If you would like to receive a free copy of our general catalogue or
details of our new publications, please fill out the enclosed postcard
and return it to us by mail or fax.

CATALOGE UND INFORMATIONEN ÜBER NEUE TITLE
Wenn Sie unseren Gesamtkatalog oder Detailinformationen über
unsere neuen Titel wünschen, fullen Sie bitte die beigefügte Postkarte
aus und schicken Sie sie uns per Post oder Fax.

ピエ・ブックス
〒170 東京都豊島区駒込 4-14-6-301
TEL: 03-3949-5010 FAX: 03-3949-5650

P·I·E BOOKS
#301, 4-14-6, Komagome, Toshima-ku, Tokyo 170 JAPAN
TEL: 03-3949-5010 FAX: 03-3949-5650